3-STEP EXPRESS
COMFORT FOOD

W9-BKQ-426

3-STEP EXPRESS
COMFORT FOOD

hearty favorites
for weeknight
cravings

table of contents

Sirloin Steaks with Mushroom Sauce, page 55

HELPFUL FEATURES

PREP TIP

Recipe-specific tips to guide you along the way

SIMPLE SWAP

Look for these suggestions for tailoring the recipes for your family's tastes or for the ingredients you have on hand

TO GO

Suggestions for enjoying it at another meal, perhaps for lunch tomorrow

SERVE WITH

Easy ideas to complete the meal

WELCOME!

Busy schedules can play havoc with serving healthy meals, especially if you want something quick and comforting. Whether you're a beginner in the kitchen or a seasoned cook, you need dinnertime solutions your family will enjoy. At *Cooking Light*, we've made it possible to create great meals with short ingredient lists and quick-cooking techniques, the mainstay of *3-Step Express*.

Think of your favorite comfort foods—meat loaf, chicken and dumplings, fried chicken, shrimp and grits, mac and cheese, tomato soup—the list goes on. We've streamlined the steps, but not the flavors, or the comfort you'll feel when enjoying these favorites.

Start by prepping your pantry with a few basic ingredients, and you'll find that even your shopping trips will be easier, leading to fewer mad dashes to the store at dinnertime. Whether friends are stopping by or you're cooking for family, these easy meals deliver big, bold flavors and won't exhaust the cook. Short ingredient lists and less than 15 minutes hands-on prep put less stress on you, making meals more enjoyable. Savor the flavors of your favorite foods and the comforts of home-cooked meals.

—the editors of *Cooking Light*

*Ham and Spinach Focaccia
Sandwiches, page 164*

Creole Chicken and Vegetables, page 32

1

express kitchen guide

The secret to mastering *3-STEP EXPRESS* meals is to stock your kitchen with the right ingredients.

STRAIGHT FROM THE PANTRY

Keep these staple ingredients on hand so quick
weeknight meals are within reach.

ORZO
This small pasta, about the size
of puffed rice grains, cooks
quickly. You can turn almost any
pasta salad into a quick-cooking
dish by substituting orzo.

STORE-BOUGHT CRUSTS
Prebaked crusts from makers such as Boboli
and Mama Mary's will cut significant time from
your prep work. Simply add your favorite
toppings for a quick pizza night.

BOIL-IN-THE-BAG RICE
No more boiling over the rice or burning it as it cooks.
Simply place the bag of white or whole-grain brown
rice in boiling water and heat. Other options include
pre-cooked rice, such as Uncle Ben's Ready Rice,
which heats in just 90 seconds in the microwave. This
version offers basmati, brown basmati, jasmine, long-
grain, and long-grain and wild-rice options.

CHOPPED CHILES
Canned chiles can make a ho-hum dish
much more exciting. While commonly used
in enchiladas and other Southwestern dishes,
canned chiles go mainstream in eggs, soups,
and casseroles. Stir them into chopped tomatoes and cilantro for a quick salsa or sauté with
vegetables for a spicy side dish.

TOMATO PASTE
This thick, rich paste is made by
cooking tomatoes for several hours,
creating concentrated flavor. If a recipe
calls for only a tablespoon or two, drop
the leftover by tablespoons onto a
parchment-lined baking sheet and freeze.
Transfer to a freezer bag, and freeze for
future use. It's also available in a tube to
simply squeeze out what you need.

PASTA

Dried pastas are certainly convenient—they're ready in about 15 minutes. Have a selection of your favorite shapes in the pantry—the smaller, thinner varieties cook more quickly. Pasta keepa indefinitely in an airtight container.

GARBANZO BEANS

For a quick source of protein, keep reduced-sodium garbanzo beans (chickpeas) on hand. Toss them with pastas, stir into soups, or add to salads.

CANNED TOMATOES

Crushed, diced, stewed, and whole tomatoes are handy for the quick cook. Also try fire-roasted tomatoes, tomatoes with basil, and tomatoes with chiles.

GNOCCHI

These small dumplings, made of flour and potatoes, can be found vacuum-packed near the pastas in your grocery. They can be boiled in just a couple of minutes, and then added to casseroles, or sautéed with a little olive oil for a quick side dish.

FLOUR TORTILLAS

No longer limited to quesadillas, flour tortillas can be topped with sauce and turned into a pizza crust, baked over an inverted glass bowl to create a salad "shell," cut into wedges and baked for chips, or cut into strips and cooked in broth to create dumplings.

JUMP-START CONVENIENCE

These easy add-ins are the secret to creating satisfying dishes with minimal effort!

BOTTLED GRATED GINGER

With just the turn of the lid of bottled ginger, you have fresh ginger flavor in seconds. Reach for a bottle or tube of ginger, and say good-bye to the leftover pieces of ginger root shriveling in the back of your refrigerator.

TRI-COLORED SLAW MIX

Slaw becomes an easy side dish when you start with pre-shredded cabbage. And, it makes an easy topping for sandwiches without the chopping typically required.

MIXED GREENS

Rinsing, drying, stemming, and chopping salad greens requires time. Ready-to-use spinach and greens eliminate those steps. Be sure to inspect them in the store to ensure they're fresh and in prime condition: no black spots or wilting.

REFRIGERATED PASTA

For those nights when you don't have 15 minutes to cook dried fettuccine, reach for refrigerated pasta. It's done in just a minute or two and is an essential ingredient in many comfort-food favorites.

REFRIGERATED CANNED PIZZA DOUGH

This dough isn't just for pizza, although it does make a fabulous and quick crust. To make quick calzones, roll it out, cover it with favorite toppings, fold it over, and bake at 425° for 10 to 12 minutes.

ONIONS

Onions are available chopped or sliced in white and purple varieties. What's the best part? No more tears from stinging eyes when cutting fresh onions.

REFRIGERATED POTATOES

Refrigerated mashed, shredded, and wedges of potatoes become the cornerstone of many comfort recipes. Look for them in the produce, meat, or dairy section of your grocery store. They are ready to heat in the microwave, brown in a skillet, or roast in the oven.

REFRIGERATED PESTO

Creamier and brighter in color than the jarred shelf-stable version, stir refrigerated pesto into a pasta sauce or soups, or toss with pastas for a jolt of fresh basil, Parmesan, and pine-nut flavor.

PRECHOPPED VEGETABLES

Look for onions, bell peppers, broccoli, zucchini, and more in the produce section to speed up any recipe.

MINCED GARLIC

Bottled ready-to-use garlic is available in most groceries. Simply use 1 teaspoon for each clove of garlic in the recipe. Once opened, store in your fridge for up to several months.

FLAVOR BOOSTS

Keep these everyday pantry items on hand so you can quickly and easily boost the flavor of almost any type of dish.

SOY SAUCE AND FISH SAUCE

Add lower-sodium soy sauce to meat loaf, burgers, steak, chicken, and barbecue sauces. Fish sauce has been called "the soy sauce of Southeast Asia." It's pungent in the bottle but mellows gorgeously when heated.

HOISIN SAUCE

This thick condiment is made from sweet potatoes, wheat, or rice mixed with vinegar, sweeteners, and lots of aromatics. Although its name means "seafood paste" in Cantonese, there's no seafood in the mix.

DIJON MUSTARD

No longer just a sandwich condiment, it can emulsify a vinaigrette or thicken a stew. Rub it on meat or fish before baking for flavor or use it to help adhere breading to baked pork or fish. It also adds tang to potato salad or mashed potatoes. You'll appreciate so much flavor from just one ingredient.

SEA SALT

A coarse-grained sea salt will offer crunch to a dry rub for meats, often a nice touch on the grill, particularly in fast-cooked items like fish fillets.

WORCESTERSHIRE SAUCE

The main ingredients include vinegar, molasses, tamarind, hot chiles, anchovies, and a warming spice like clove or cinnamon. It's the ideal grab-and-use seasoning, as it contains all the flavor components, sweet and salty, spicy and sour. Add it to marinades, meat loaf, and other beef dishes, or drizzle it over sautéed vegetables at the end of cooking for that "something extra" flavor.

HOT CHILI SAUCE

This bottled condiment, a blend of chiles and vinegar, is a Southeast Asian favorite. Sriracha is smooth and sweet like ketchup (but much hotter).

BALSAMIC VINEGAR

A perfect pantry has two types of balsamic vinegar: the syrupy, aged stuff to drizzle over steamed vegetables and a more economical bottling to use in sauces and marinades.

CRUSHED RED PEPPER AND PEPPERCORNS

These lend a kick to dishes from meats and vegetables to soups and pizzas. Keep a peppermill on hand and give a twist to unlock the freshly ground flavor on a mixed green salad or pasta dish.

RED WINE VINEGAR

This flavor booster can be used for deglazing pans, boosting the flavor of marinades, and adding depth to sauces. Try it drizzled over berry desserts or splashed over roasted meats.

STOCKING THE FREEZER

Fill your freezer with meat and veggies. Those mad-dash runs to the grocery won't be needed, as you'll always have star ingredients on hand.

FROZEN MIXED VEGETABLES

Frozen veggies are ideal for getting dinner on the table in minutes. They retain not only their nutrients but also much of their sweet flavor. Steam them in the microwave for a quick-cooking side, sauté with fresh herbs for an easy stovetop option, and add them to soups and casseroles. The options are endless!

FROZEN CHOPPED ONION, CELERY, AND PEPPERS

No need to thaw before cooking. Just measure, add to the recipe, and cook according to the directions. Freeze up to 8 months.

FROZEN CHICKEN BREASTS, THIGHS, AND TENDERS

Quick-thaw frozen skinless, boneless chicken to cook for sandwiches and entrées or to add to soups and casseroles.

FROZEN PEELED AND DEVEINED SHRIMP

Shrimp can be thawed quickly in cold water or overnight in the refrigerator, ready to sauté, grill, or cook to add to pastas and casseroles. Frozen shrimp that have already been peeled and deveined are available in one-pound bags, saving you at least 10 minutes of prep.

TEN TIPS

for preparing 3-step express meals

1 Make a Game Plan
Read through the recipe before starting to see what needs to be chopped prior to cooking. Some chopping and prepping can be done while foods are browning or cooking, which keeps the time to a minimum.

2 Read Ahead, Stay Ahead
As you work your way through the steps, continue to read ahead. For many recipes you can begin the next step while the current step simmers.

3 Gathering Saves Time
Gather all ingredients before beginning to cook to avoid stopping and hunting for items midway through the recipe.

4 Easy Bird, Easy Meals
For recipes calling for chopped cooked chicken, you can start with a rotisserie chicken from the grocery and pull the chicken from the bone right after you purchase it. The meat will be easier to pull while it's still warm. Go ahead and chop or shred it, then store it in the refrigerator for a quick weeknight meal.

5 More Chicken Options
On the weekends or when you have the time, cook extra chicken breasts or roast a whole bird. Store the cooked meat in the refrigerator if using in the next few days or in an airtight container in the freezer for future use. Simply pull out what you need for quesadillas, soups, and casseroles for a jump start on meals throughout the week.

6 Avoid the Crowd
When browning meats, use larger skillets and don't overcrowd the pan. You'll also appreciate the ease of turning the food in a larger pan.

7 Divide for Quickness
For roasted vegetables, divide between two rimmed baking sheets for a quicker cook time and for proper roasting rather than overcrowded steaming.

8 Double and Save Time
Double the amount of rice or pasta and save the leftovers for a quick salad during the week ahead.

9 Chop Ahead
When you chop one onion, chop two. You can chop two onions more quickly than you can chop one on two separate occasions. Scoop the second chopped onion into a zip-top plastic bag, and store it in the freezer for a future meal. The same goes for celery, carrots, and bell peppers.

10 Small Is Fast
Almost all long-cooking vegetables can be quick-cookers if they are cut into small bits. The prime example is carrots, added to many a quick sauté once they are sliced into paper-thin coins or shredded through the large holes of a box grater. You can purchase shredded carrots for added convenience.

Spicy Honey-Brushed Chicken Thighs, page 36

2

poultry & meat »

Escape the dinnertime rut with these fresh flavors. You'll discover that ease is the key for meals the family will enjoy.

Chicken *and* Dumplings

HANDS-ON TIME: 15 min. **TOTAL TIME:** 20 min.

 PREP TIP *Keep the tortillas stacked together, and then cut the entire stack into strips at one time.*

1 tablespoon butter
½ cup prechopped onion
2 cups chopped roasted skinless, boneless chicken breast
1 (10-ounce) box frozen mixed vegetables, thawed
1½ cups water
1 tablespoon all-purpose flour

1 (14-ounce) can fat-free, lower-sodium chicken broth
¼ teaspoon salt
¼ teaspoon black pepper
1 bay leaf
8 (6-inch) flour tortillas, cut into ½-inch-wide strips
1 tablespoon chopped fresh parsley

 **Melt butter** in a large saucepan over medium-high heat. Add onion; sauté 5 minutes or until tender. Stir in chicken and vegetables; cook 3 minutes or until thoroughly heated, stirring constantly.

 While chicken mixture cooks, combine 1½ cups water, flour, and broth. Gradually stir broth mixture into chicken mixture. Stir in salt, pepper, and bay leaf; bring to a boil. Reduce heat, and simmer 3 minutes.

 Stir in tortilla strips, and cook 2 minutes or until tortilla strips soften. Remove from heat; stir in parsley. Discard bay leaf. Serve immediately. Serves 4 (serving size: about 1½ cups)

Calories 366; Fat 9.3g (sat 3.1g, mono 3.9g, poly 1.4g); Protein 29.8g; Carb 40.3g; Fiber 5.3g; Chol 67mg; Iron 3.4mg; Sodium 652mg; Calc 104mg

 SIMPLE SWAP **Leftover roasted turkey is an easy substitution for the chicken in this recipe.**

Chicken Parmigiana *(pictured on page 2)*

HANDS-ON TIME: 6 min. **TOTAL TIME:** 36 min.

 PREP TIP *Be sure to add the cheese during the last five minutes of baking so it's just melted and not burned. For an extra kick of flavor, use red pepper in the flour mixture.*

1.5 ounces all-purpose flour (¹/₃ cup)

¹/₄ teaspoon garlic powder

¹/₄ teaspoon paprika

¹/₄ teaspoon pepper

2 egg whites, lightly beaten

6 (4-ounce) skinless, boneless chicken breast halves

2 cups cornflakes, coarsely crushed

Cooking spray

1 (26-ounce) jar low-fat pasta sauce (such as Healthy Choice)

3 ounces preshredded part-skim mozzarella cheese (about ³/₄ cup)

 1 **Preheat oven to 350°.** Combine first 4 ingredients in a shallow dish. Place egg whites in a shallow dish. Place cornflakes in a shallow dish. Dredge each chicken breast in flour mixture. Dip each breast in egg whites; dredge in cornflakes.

 2 **Arrange chicken in a 13 x 9-inch baking dish** coated with cooking spray. Bake at 350° for 25 minutes or until crisp.

3 **While chicken bakes,** place pasta sauce in a medium saucepan, and cook over medium heat until thoroughly heated. Pour sauce over chicken, and sprinkle with cheese. Bake an additional 5 minutes or until cheese melts. Serves 6 (serving size: 1 chicken breast half and ¹/₂ cup sauce)

Calories 273; Fat 4.4g (sat 1.8g, mono 1g, poly 0.4g); Protein 34.1g; Carb 22.5g; Fiber 2.3g; Chol 74mg; Iron 1.7mg; Sodium 596mg; Calc 107mg

 SERVE WITH *Serve over pasta for a complete meal—perfect for kids and weeknight dinners in a hurry.*

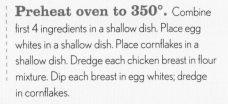

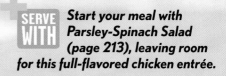

SERVE WITH *Start your meal with Parsley-Spinach Salad (page 213), leaving room for this full-flavored chicken entrée.*

Balsamic Chicken

HANDS-ON TIME: 8 min. **TOTAL TIME:** 33 min.

 This is a lazy-day dish reserved for when you really don't feel like cooking or shopping. Keep all the staples in the pantry, and the chicken breasts and vegetables in the fridge or freezer.

½ cup instant rice
1 teaspoon olive oil
¾ cup prechopped onion
4 garlic cloves, sliced
2 (4-ounce) skinless, boneless chicken breast halves
1 cup prechopped green bell pepper
½ cup balsamic vinegar
¼ cup presliced mushrooms
1 teaspoon dried Italian seasoning
1 (14.5-ounce) can diced tomatoes, undrained
2 teaspoons sliced green onions

1 **Cook rice** according to package directions, omitting salt and fat.

2 **While rice cooks, heat a large skillet** over medium-high heat. Add oil to pan; swirl to coat. Add ¾ cup onion and garlic; sauté 3 minutes. Add chicken; cook 4 minutes on each side or until browned.

3 **Add bell pepper and remaining ingredients,** except green onions. Reduce heat to medium-low; cook 20 minutes or until chicken is done. Serve over rice, and sprinkle with green onions. Serves 2 (serving size: 1 chicken breast half, 1 cup bell pepper mixture, and ½ cup rice)

Calories 376; Fat 4.3g (sat 0.8g, mono 2.1g, poly 0.7g); Protein 32g; Carb 52.3g; Fiber 6g; Chol 66mg; Iron 3.8mg; Sodium 355mg; Calc 110mg

 SIMPLE SWAP **Sneak leftover vegetables into this quick dish. Use spinach, zucchini, mushrooms, and green onions—they all taste great.**

Pan-Grilled Chicken *with* Vegetable Relish *(pictured on cover)*

HANDS-ON TIME: 5 min. **TOTAL TIME:** 14 min.

 PREP TIP *Be sure to dice the carrot, not chop, as the smaller pieces will cook faster.*

4 (6-ounce) skinless, boneless chicken breast halves

½ teaspoon kosher salt, divided

¼ teaspoon freshly ground black pepper

Cooking spray

¼ cup sliced onion

¼ cup diced carrot

¼ cup prechopped yellow bell pepper

¼ cup prechopped red bell pepper

¼ cup prechopped green bell pepper

¼ cup fat-free, lower-sodium chicken broth

1 tablespoon chopped fresh cilantro

 Heat a grill pan over medium-high heat. Sprinkle chicken with ¼ teaspoon salt and pepper. Coat pan with cooking spray. Add chicken to pan; cook 6 minutes on each side or until done.

 While chicken cooks, heat a large skillet over medium-high heat. Add onion and carrot; cook 2 minutes, stirring occasionally. Add bell peppers and ¼ teaspoon salt; cook 1 minute or until crisp-tender.

Add broth; cook 2 minutes or until liquid almost evaporates, scraping pan to loosen browned bits. Spoon vegetable mixture over chicken; top with cilantro. Serves 4 (serving size: 1 breast half and ¼ cup relish)

Calories 214; Fat 5g (sat 1.1g, mono 1.7g, poly 0.8g); Protein 36.74g; Carb 3.3g; Fiber 0.9g; Chol 109mg; Iron 0.8mg; Sodium 480mg; Calc 16mg

 SERVE WITH *Serve with grilled garlic bread and a mixed green salad. Toss sliced cucumber and radish with the salad for extra crunch.*

Parmesan Chicken *and* Rice

HANDS-ON TIME: 10 min. **TOTAL TIME:** 18 min.

 PREP TIP *Use a large nonstick skillet so there'll be room to stir in the rice and broth. Purchase fresh Parmesan cheese that's already grated.*

1 tablespoon olive oil

½ cup prechopped onion

1 teaspoon bottled minced garlic

2 teaspoons fresh thyme

1 (8-ounce) package presliced mushrooms

¾ pound skinless, boneless chicken breast, cut into bite-sized pieces

½ cup dry white wine

½ teaspoon salt

¼ teaspoon freshly ground black pepper

1 cup uncooked instant rice

1 cup fat-free, lower-sodium chicken broth

2 ounces grated fresh Parmesan cheese (about ½ cup)

¼ cup chopped fresh parsley

1 **Heat a large nonstick skillet** over medium-high heat. Add oil to pan; swirl to coat. Add onion, garlic, thyme, and mushrooms; sauté 5 minutes or until onion is tender.

2 **Add chicken;** sauté 4 minutes or until the chicken is lightly browned. Add wine, salt, and pepper; cook 3 minutes or until liquid almost evaporates.

3 **Stir in rice and broth.** Bring to a boil; cover, reduce heat, and simmer 5 minutes or until liquid is absorbed. Stir in cheese and parsley. Serves 4 (serving size: about 1 cup)

Calories 351; Fat 10.7g (sat 1.3g, mono 2.8g, poly 3.8g); Protein 14.8g; Carb 55.5g; Fiber 10.2g; Chol 57mg; Iron 7.3mg; Sodium 489mg; Calc 338mg

 SIMPLE SWAP A sweet white wine can be used in place of a dry wine for a subtle hint of sweetness.

SERVE WITH ***Serve these saucy orange-topped chicken breast halves with Asian noodles—such as soba, somen, or udon—and steamed snow peas.***

Orange Mandarin Chicken

HANDS-ON TIME: 8 min. **TOTAL TIME:** 16 min.

 Chop the green onions and jalapeño while the chicken cooks. Combine the cornstarch, broth, and soy sauce before adding it to the hot pan to keep the sauce smooth.

- **2 teaspoons dark sesame oil**
- **4 (4-ounce) skinless, boneless chicken breast halves**
- **½ teaspoon salt**
- **¼ teaspoon freshly ground black pepper**
- **1 (11-ounce) can mandarin oranges in light syrup, undrained**
- **½ cup chopped green onions**
- **1 tablespoon finely chopped seeded red and green jalapeño pepper**
- **1 teaspoon bottled minced garlic**
- **½ cup fat-free, lower-sodium chicken broth**
- **1 tablespoon lower-sodium soy sauce**
- **2 teaspoons cornstarch**

1 **Heat a large nonstick skillet** over medium-high heat. Add oil to pan; swirl to coat. Sprinkle chicken with salt and pepper. Add chicken to pan; cook 4 minutes on each side or until browned.

2 **While chicken cooks,** drain oranges in a colander over a bowl, reserving 2 tablespoons liquid. Add oranges, 2 tablespoons liquid, onions, jalapeño, and garlic to pan. Reduce heat; simmer 2 minutes.

3 **Combine broth, soy sauce, and cornstarch;** add to pan. Bring to a boil; cook 1 minute or until slightly thickened. Serves 4 (serving size: 1 chicken breast half and 6 tablespoons sauce)

Calories 212; Fat 3.8g (sat 0.7g, mono 1.3g, poly 1.3g); Protein 27.2g; Carb 15.2g; Fiber 0.7g; Chol 66mg; Iron 1.9mg; Sodium 562mg; Calc 27mg

 SIMPLE SWAP **One pound pork cutlets or thin boneless pork chops can be used instead of the chicken. Depending on the thickness, cook 3 minutes on each side or until done.**

Chicken Fried Rice

HANDS-ON TIME: 19 min. **TOTAL TIME:** 19 min.

 PREP TIP *Save time by doing two steps at once: While the water for the rice heats, cut the chicken and measure the seasonings.*

2 (3½-ounce) bags boil-in-bag long-grain white rice

7 teaspoons lower-sodium soy sauce, divided

1 teaspoon cornstarch

12 ounces skinless, boneless chicken breast halves, cut into ½-inch pieces

2 tablespoons hoisin sauce

2 tablespoons rice wine vinegar

2 tablespoons fresh lime juice

1 teaspoon chili paste with garlic

2 tablespoons canola oil, divided

2 large eggs, lightly beaten

1 cup prechopped white onion

1 teaspoon bottled ground fresh ginger (such as Spice World)

1 tablespoon bottled minced garlic

1 cup frozen green peas, thawed

½ cup chopped green onions

1 **Cook rice** according to package directions, omitting salt and fat.

2 **While rice cooks,** combine 1 tablespoon soy sauce, cornstarch, and chicken in a bowl; toss well. Combine remaining 4 teaspoons soy sauce, hoisin sauce, and next 3 ingredients (through chili paste) in a small bowl.

3 **Heat a wok** or large nonstick skillet over medium-high heat. Add 1 tablespoon oil to pan; swirl to coat. Add chicken mixture; stir-fry 4 minutes or until lightly browned. Push chicken to one side of skillet; add eggs to open side of pan. Cook 45 seconds, stirring constantly; stir eggs and chicken mixture together. Remove chicken mixture from pan; keep warm. Return pan to medium-high heat. Add 1 tablespoon oil to pan. Add white onion, ginger, and garlic; cook 2 minutes or until fragrant. Add rice; cook 1 minute. Add peas; cook 1 minute. Add chicken mixture and soy sauce mixture; cook 2 minutes or until thoroughly heated. Remove pan from heat; stir in green onions. Serves 4 (serving size: about 1½ cups)

Calories 477; Fat 11.7g (sat 1.7g, mono 5.7g, poly 2.7g); Protein 30.2g; Carb 58.3g; Fiber 3.5g; Chol 139mg; Iron 3.5mg; Sodium 488mg; Calc 58mg

 SERVE WITH *Serve with Asian Slaw (page 215), and enjoy a fortune cookie at the end of the meal.*

Sweet *and* Sour Chicken

HANDS-ON TIME: 15 min. **TOTAL TIME:** 15 min.

 PREP TIP *To speed preparation time, cut the chicken into pieces while you wait for the pan to heat.*

- 1 tablespoon olive oil
- 1 tablespoon bottled minced garlic
- 1 teaspoon bottled ground fresh ginger (such as Spice World)
- 1/4 teaspoon crushed red pepper
- 1 1/2 pounds skinless, boneless chicken breast, cut into 1/2-inch pieces
- 1 (16-ounce) package frozen pepper stir-fry with onion

- 1 (15 1/4-ounce) can pineapple chunks in juice, undrained
- 1/3 cup lower-sodium soy sauce
- 2 tablespoons dry sherry
- 1 1/2 tablespoons cornstarch
- 2 teaspoons brown sugar
- 1/4 cup unsalted dry-roasted chopped cashews

1 **Heat** a large nonstick skillet over medium-high heat. Add oil to pan; swirl to coat. Add garlic, ginger, red pepper, and chicken to pan; sauté 5 minutes or until chicken is done. Remove chicken mixture from pan; set aside.

2 **Add pepper stir-fry to pan;** sauté 4 minutes or until crisp-tender. Drain pineapple, reserving 1/2 cup juice. Add 1 cup pineapple chunks to pan; cook 30 seconds. Reserve remaining pineapple for another use. Combine reserved 1/2 cup juice, soy sauce, sherry, cornstarch, and sugar in a bowl, stirring with a whisk until smooth.

3 **Return chicken mixture to pan.** Stir in juice mixture; bring to boil. Cook 1 minute. Sprinkle with cashews. Serves 4 (serving size: about 1 cup)

Calories 388; Fat 11.6g (sat 2.4g, mono 6.2g, poly 2g); Protein 41.5g; Carb 28.9g; Fiber 2.1g; Chol 101mg; Iron 2.7mg; Sodium 551mg; Calc 58mg

 SIMPLE SWAP You can use 2 cups chopped onion, celery, and green bell pepper in place of the frozen stir-fry vegetables.

+ SERVE WITH Serve with steamed green beans. Two 8-ounce packages of microwave steam-in-bag green beans will produce an almost-effortless side.

30

Chicken *with* Honey-Beer Sauce

HANDS-ON TIME: 5 min. **TOTAL TIME:** 20 min.

 PREP TIP *Opt for an inexpensive, full-flavored domestic beer, like Blue Moon wheat ale.*

- **2 teaspoons canola oil**
- **4 (6-ounce) skinless, boneless chicken breast halves**
- **¼ teaspoon freshly ground black pepper**
- **⅛ teaspoon salt**
- **3 tablespoons thinly sliced shallots**
- **½ cup beer**
- **2 tablespoons lower-sodium soy sauce**
- **1 tablespoon whole-grain Dijon mustard**
- **1 tablespoon honey**
- **2 tablespoons flat-leaf parsley leaves**

 Heat a large skillet over medium-high heat. Add oil to pan; swirl to coat. Sprinkle chicken evenly with pepper and salt. Add chicken to pan; sauté 6 minutes on each side or until done. Remove chicken from pan; keep warm.

 Add shallots to pan; cook 1 minute or until translucent. Combine beer and next 3 ingredients (through honey) in a small bowl; stir with a whisk. Add beer mixture to pan; bring to a boil, scraping pan to loosen browned bits. Cook 3 minutes or until liquid is reduced to ½ cup.

3 Return chicken to pan; turn to coat with sauce. Sprinkle evenly with parsley. Serves 4 (serving size: 1 breast half and 2 tablespoons sauce)

Calories 245; Fat 4.5g (sat 0.7g, mono 2g, poly 1.1g); Protein 40g; Carb 7.8g; Fiber 0.2g; Chol 99mg; Iron 1.6mg; Sodium 544mg; Calc 27mg

 SIMPLE SWAP Use chicken thighs or tenderloins—whatever you have on hand.

Creole Chicken *and* Vegetables *(pictured on page 8)*

HANDS-ON TIME: 11 min. **TOTAL TIME:** 19 min.

 PREP TIP *Keep the frozen pepper stir-fry on hand, as it's an easy way to boost the vegetables in a dish without any prep.*

Cooking spray
1 pound chicken breast tenders
2 cups frozen pepper stir-fry (such as Birds Eye), thawed
1 cup frozen cut okra, thawed
3/4 cup thinly sliced celery
3/4 teaspoon sugar
1/2 teaspoon salt
1/2 teaspoon dried thyme
1/4 teaspoon ground red pepper
1 (14.5-ounce) can diced tomatoes, undrained
1/4 cup chopped fresh parsley
1 tablespoon butter

 1 **Heat a large** nonstick skillet over medium-high heat. Coat pan with cooking spray. Add chicken; cook 3 minutes on each side or until browned.

 2 **Add pepper stir-fry** and next 6 ingredients (through red pepper), stirring to combine. Pour tomatoes over chicken mixture; bring to a boil.

3 **Cover, reduce heat, and simmer** 5 minutes. Uncover; cook 3 minutes. Add parsley and butter, stirring until butter melts. Serves 4 (serving size: 1 cup)

Calories 199; Fat 4.4g (sat 1.8g, mono 1.5g, poly 0.5g); Protein 28.3g; Carb 11g; Fiber 3.2g; Chol 73mg; Iron 1.9mg; Sodium 550mg; Calc 71mg

 SIMPLE SWAP Frozen peppers and okra make this speedy, but you can use fresh if they're in season.

Coconut Chicken Fingers

HANDS-ON TIME: 15 min. **TOTAL TIME:** 15 min.

 A tasty gluten-free option, this recipe uses rice flour instead of wheat flour for the coating, however all-purpose flour may also be used.

24 **ounces chicken breast tenders**
½ **teaspoon salt**
¼ **teaspoon ground red pepper**
1 **cup rice flour**
1 **cup whole buttermilk**

1 **large egg**
1½ **cups unsweetened flaked coconut**
3 **tablespoons canola oil**
Sweet chile sauce (optional)

1 **Sprinkle chicken** with salt and pepper. Place flour in a shallow dish. Combine buttermilk and egg in a shallow dish, stirring well. Place coconut in a shallow dish.

2 **Dredge chicken in flour;** shake off excess. Dip chicken in egg mixture; dredge in coconut.

3 **Heat a large skillet** over medium-high heat. Add oil to pan; swirl to coat. Add chicken to pan; cook 6 minutes or until done, turning to brown. Serve with chile sauce, if desired. Serves 6 (serving size: about 4½ ounces)

Calories 298; Fat 12.7g (sat 4.1g, mono 5.4g, poly 2.6g); Protein 28.7g; Carb 15.9g; Fiber 1.7g; Chol 102mg; Iron 1.4mg; Sodium 318mg; Calc 20mg

+ *Sweet chile sauce is a favorite dipping sauce. And kids will also love the sweetness that the coconut adds to the coating of these chicken fingers. Serve with Steamed Sugar Snap Peas (page 209), cooking the peas during step 3 of the chicken.*

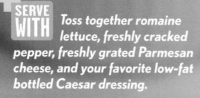

+ SERVE WITH *Toss together romaine lettuce, freshly cracked pepper, freshly grated Parmesan cheese, and your favorite low-fat bottled Caesar dressing.*

Chicken Potpies

HANDS-ON TIME: 11 min. **TOTAL TIME:** 24 min.

 PREP TIP *Because the piecrust topping cooks on a baking sheet and is then placed over the filling, you don't need to use ovenproof bowls for the pies. Use a bowl or ramekin as a guide for cutting the dough.*

½ (15-ounce) package refrigerated pie dough (such as Pillsbury)

Cooking spray

2 tablespoons all-purpose flour

1 teaspoon dried rubbed sage

¼ teaspoon salt

¼ teaspoon black pepper

8 ounces chicken breast tenders, cut into bite-sized pieces

1¼ cups water

1½ cups frozen mixed vegetables

1 cup mushrooms, quartered

⅔ cup light chive and onion cream cheese

1 cup fat-free, lower-sodium chicken broth

 Preheat oven to 425°.

 Cut 4 (4-inch) circles out of dough; discard remaining dough. Place dough circles on a baking sheet coated with cooking spray. Lightly coat dough with cooking spray. Pierce top of dough with a fork. Bake at 425° for 8 minutes or until golden.

 While the crust bakes, combine flour, sage, salt, and pepper in a zip-top plastic bag; add chicken. Seal bag, and toss to coat. Heat a large nonstick skillet over medium-high heat. Add chicken mixture, and coat with cooking spray; cook 5 minutes, browning on all sides. Stir in 1¼ cups water, scraping pan to loosen browned bits. Stir in vegetables, mushrooms, cream cheese, and broth; bring to a boil. Reduce heat, and cook 8 minutes. Spoon 1 cup chicken mixture into each of 4 (1-cup) ramekins or bowls; top each serving with 1 piecrust. Serves 4 (serving size: 1 pie)

Calories 339; Fat 12.4g (sat 6.1g, mono 4.7g, poly 0.3g); Protein 20.2g; Carb 27.71g; Fiber 1.4g; Chol 60mg; Iron 0.7mg; Sodium 768mg; Calc 155mg

 SIMPLE SWAP **You can use 2 cups chopped leftover chicken in place of chicken breast tenders.**

Spicy Honey-Brushed Chicken Thighs *(pictured on page 18)*

HANDS-ON TIME: 6 min. **TOTAL TIME:** 16 min.

 PREP TIP *Turn on the broiler the minute you get into the kitchen so that it will be ready when you are.*

2 teaspoons garlic powder
2 teaspoons chili powder
1 teaspoon ground cumin
1 teaspoon paprika
½ teaspoon salt
½ teaspoon ground red pepper
8 skinless, boneless chicken thighs
Cooking spray
6 tablespoons honey
2 teaspoons cider vinegar

1 Preheat broiler. Combine first 6 ingredients in a large bowl. Add chicken to bowl; toss to coat.

2 Place chicken on a broiler pan coated with cooking spray. Broil chicken 5 minutes on each side.

3 Combine honey and vinegar in a small bowl, stirring well. Remove chicken from oven; brush ¼ cup honey mixture on chicken. Broil 1 minute. Remove chicken from oven, and turn over. Brush chicken with remaining honey mixture. Broil 1 additional minute or until chicken is done. Serves 4 (serving size: 2 chicken thighs)

Calories 321; Fat 11g (sat 3g, mono 4.1g, poly 2.5g); Protein 28g; Carb 27.9g; Fiber 0.6g; Chol 99mg; Iron 2.1mg; Sodium 386mg; Calc 21mg

 SERVE WITH *Serve with garlic-roasted potato wedges and a salad or steamed Broccolini.*

Roasted Chicken Thighs *with* Mustard-Thyme Sauce

HANDS-ON TIME: 14 min. **TOTAL TIME:** 25 min.

The tasty browned bits that remain behind after the chicken cooks become the basis of the speedy sauce. Serve with roasted potatoes and haricots verts (French green beans).

1 tablespoon olive oil

8 bone-in chicken thighs, skinned (about 2½ pounds)

½ teaspoon salt, divided

½ teaspoon freshly ground black pepper, divided

1 tablespoon butter

½ cup prechopped onion

2 teaspoons chopped fresh thyme

1 cup no-salt-added chicken stock (such as Swanson), divided

4 teaspoons flour

1 teaspoon Dijon mustard

1 **Preheat** oven to 425°. Heat a large nonstick skillet over medium-high heat. Add oil to pan; swirl to coat. Sprinkle chicken with ¼ teaspoon salt and ¼ teaspoon pepper. Add chicken to pan; cook 4 minutes on each side or until lightly browned.

2 **Place chicken** in an 11 x 7-inch glass or ceramic baking dish. Bake at 425° for 16 minutes or until a thermometer registers 165°. Remove chicken from dish; remove and reserve drippings.

3 **Return skillet** to medium-high heat. Add butter; swirl to coat. Add onion and thyme; sauté 5 minutes or until tender. Combine 3 tablespoons stock and flour in a small bowl, stirring with a whisk until smooth. Add flour mixture, remaining stock, and reserved drippings to pan, scraping pan to loosen browned bits. Bring to a boil, and cook 2 minutes or until slightly thickened. Remove from heat, and add mustard, ¼ teaspoon salt, and ¼ teaspoon pepper, stirring with a whisk. Serve sauce with chicken. Serves 4 (serving size: 2 thighs and 3 tablespoons sauce)

Calories 246; Fat 11.7g (sat 3.7g, mono 4.9g, poly 1.8g); Protein 28.9g; Carb 4.6g; Fiber 0.5g; Chol 122mg; Iron 1.8mg; Sodium 498mg; Calc 27mg

Chicken *and* Kielbasa Rice

HANDS-ON TIME: 15 min. **TOTAL TIME:** 15 min.

PREP TIP *No need to wait for the broth mixture to come to a boil before starting step 2. You'll save minutes this way.*

2 cups fat-free, lower-sodium chicken broth

⅛ teaspoon ground turmeric

8 ounces turkey kielbasa, cut into ½-inch pieces

2 cups long-grain parboiled rice (such as Uncle Ben's)

2 teaspoons olive oil

8 ounces skinless, boneless chicken thighs, cut into bite-sized pieces

1 cup prechopped onion

1 cup prechopped green bell pepper

½ cup frozen green peas

¼ cup sliced pitted reduced-salt stuffed manzanilla (or green) olives

1 tablespoon bottled minced garlic

1 Combine first 3 ingredients in a medium saucepan; bring to a boil. Stir in rice. Cover, reduce heat, and simmer 5 minutes. Remove from heat; let stand 5 minutes.

2 While rice cooks, heat a large skillet over high heat. Add oil to pan; swirl to coat. Add chicken; cook 2 minutes or until browned, stirring occasionally. Add onion and bell pepper; sauté 4 minutes or until tender.

3 Stir in peas, olives, and garlic; sauté 1 minute. Add rice mixture; cook 1 minute or until thoroughly heated, stirring constantly. Serves 4 (serving size: 1½ cups)

Calories 428; Fat 11.5g (sat 2.6g, mono 5.4g, poly 2.4g); Protein 26.7g; Carb 53.1g; Fiber 4g; Chol 84mg; Iron 5.2mg; Sodium 731mg; Calc 60mg

SIMPLE SWAP If you want to splurge on price, you can substitute a few crushed saffron threads for the turmeric.

Oven-Fried Chicken Thighs *with* Buttermilk-Mustard Sauce

HANDS-ON TIME: 7 min. **TOTAL TIME:** 44 min.

 PREP TIP *Don't be stopped by the total time—it includes the time the chicken chills and bakes, which is "hands-off" time for you to do other things. Preheating the baking sheet helps crisp the chicken on the bottom as it bakes.*

¹⁄₄ cup low-fat buttermilk
4 teaspoons Dijon mustard
1 tablespoon honey
¹⁄₈ teaspoon salt
¹⁄₄ teaspoon freshly ground black pepper
¹⁄₈ teaspoon dried rosemary
¹⁄₄ cup dry breadcrumbs
1¹⁄₂ tablespoons grated fresh Parmesan cheese
4 bone-in chicken thighs (about 1 pound), skinned
Cooking spray

1 **Preheat oven to 425°.** Combine first 6 ingredients in a small microwave-safe bowl. Spoon 3 tablespoons buttermilk mixture into a shallow bowl; reserve remaining mixture.

2 **Combine breadcrumbs and Parmesan cheese** in a small bowl. Dip chicken in 3 tablespoons buttermilk mixture; dredge in breadcrumb mixture. Chill 15 minutes. While chicken chills, lightly coat a baking sheet with cooking spray, and place in oven for 5 minutes.

3 **Place chicken** on heated baking sheet. Bake at 425° for 24 minutes or until a meat thermometer registers 180°, turning chicken after 12 minutes. Microwave reserved buttermilk mixture at HIGH 20 seconds or until warm. Drizzle sauce over chicken. Serves 2 (serving size: 2 thighs and 2 tablespoons sauce)

Calories 347; Fat 12g (sat 3.8g, mono 4g, poly 2.8g); Protein 37.7g; Carb 20.4g; Fiber 0.5g; Chol 129mg; Iron 2.6mg; Sodium 598mg; Calc 148mg

 SERVE WITH *Serve with Garlic-Chili Corn: Melt 1 tablespoon butter with minced garlic and a dash of chili powder in a microwave-safe bowl. Drizzle over steamed corn-on-the-cob.*

SERVE WITH *Serve with Microwave Smashed Potatoes (page 207) and Steamed Sugar Snap Peas (page 209).*

Oven-Fried Chicken

HANDS-ON TIME: 9 min. **TOTAL TIME:** 48 min.

 PREP TIP *Purchase chicken pieces for ease. For a milder version, you can substitute white pepper for the red.*

1 cup low-fat buttermilk

2 large egg whites, beaten

4.5 ounces all-purpose flour (about 1 cup)

⅓ cup cornmeal

½ teaspoon salt, divided

¾ teaspoon freshly ground black pepper

¼ teaspoon ground red pepper

2 chicken breast halves, skinned (about 1 pound)

2 chicken thighs, skinned (about ½ pound)

2 chicken drumsticks, skinned (about ½ pound)

2 tablespoons canola oil

Cooking spray

 **1 Preheat oven to 425°.** Cover a large baking sheet with parchment paper.

 2 Combine buttermilk and egg whites in a shallow dish; stir well with a whisk. Combine flour, cornmeal, ¼ teaspoon salt, black pepper, and red pepper in a separate shallow dish; stir well. Sprinkle chicken evenly with remaining ¼ teaspoon salt. Dip chicken in buttermilk mixture; dredge in flour mixture.

3 Heat a large nonstick skillet over medium-high heat. Add oil to pan; swirl to coat. Add chicken to pan; cook 4 minutes on each side or until lightly browned. Place chicken on prepared baking sheet; lightly coat chicken with cooking spray. Bake at 425° for 30 minutes or until chicken is done. Serves 4 (serving size: 1 chicken breast half, or 1 drumstick and 1 thigh).

Calories 363; Fat 12.6g (sat 2.1g, mono 5.3g, poly 3.6g); Protein 30.9g; Carb 29.9g; Fiber 1.7g; Chol 79mg; Iron 2.7mg; Sodium 295mg; Calc 50mg

 SIMPLE SWAP If you prefer white meat, use 4 chicken breast halves (about 2 pounds), skinned.

Pair this main-dish salad with toasted
buttery baguette slices: Broil 8 (1/2-inch-thick)
slices French bread baguette for 1 1/2 minutes. Turn
slices over; brush evenly with 2 tablespoons melted
butter. Broil 1 1/2 minutes or until lightly browned.

Roasted Chicken Salad

HANDS-ON TIME: 15 min. **TOTAL TIME:** 15 min.

 PREP TIP *Toast the sesame seeds quickly in a dry skillet over medium-high heat until golden, stirring frequently.*

3 tablespoons rice vinegar
1 tablespoon dark sesame oil
1/2 teaspoon crushed red pepper
1 (2 1/4-pound) whole roasted chicken, skinned
1/2 cup fresh cilantro leaves
2 tablespoons sesame seeds, toasted
1 (10-ounce) bag Italian-blend salad greens (about 6 cups)

1 **Combine first 3 ingredients**
in a large bowl; stir well, and set aside.

2 **Remove chicken from bones,**
and shred with 2 forks to measure about 4 cups meat.

3 **Add chicken, cilantro, sesame seeds, and greens**
to bowl; toss gently to coat. Serve immediately.
Serves 4 (serving size: 2 cups)

Calories 282; Fat 14.2g (sat 3.1g, mono 5.2g, poly 4.4g); Protein 34.9g; Carb 2.4g;
Fiber 0.8g; Chol 101mg; Iron 2.2mg; Sodium 458mg; Calc 29mg

 SIMPLE SWAP You can use 2 (9-ounce) packages roasted skinless, boneless chicken breast in place of the whole chicken, chopping the meat instead of shredding it.

Turkey Tenders

HANDS-ON TIME: 10 min. **TOTAL TIME:** 24 min.

 PREP TIP *The biggest difference between panko and regular breadcrumbs is that panko is coarse, giving the food a light, crunchy coating that stays crisper longer than regular breadcrumbs, however regular breadcrumbs can be substituted. The cheese adds extra flavor.*

1 **(1-pound) turkey tenderloin**
1.1 **ounces all-purpose flour (about ¼ cup)**
⅓ **cup egg substitute**
¾ **cup panko (Japanese breadcrumbs)**
2 **tablespoons grated fresh Parmesan cheese**
¼ **teaspoon garlic salt**
¼ **teaspoon freshly ground black pepper**
1 **tablespoon canola oil**
Chopped fresh flat leaf parsley (optional)

1 **Preheat oven to 425°.**
Cut tenderloin in half lengthwise; cut into 20 (2-inch) pieces.

2 **Place flour in a shallow dish.**
Place egg substitute in a shallow dish. Combine panko, cheese, garlic salt, and pepper in another dish. Dredge turkey in flour; dip in egg substitute, and dredge in breadcrumb mixture.

3 **Heat a large nonstick skillet**
over medium-high heat. Add oil to pan; swirl to coat. Add turkey pieces to pan; cook 2 minutes on each side. Place turkey pieces on a broiler pan. Bake at 425° for 5 minutes. Turn turkey pieces over, and bake an additional 5 minutes or until golden. Garnish with parsley, if desired. Serves 4 (serving size: 5 pieces)

Calories 227; Fat 6.1g (sat 1.2g, mono 2.7g, poly 1.3g); Protein 32.9g; Carb 11g; Fiber 0.5g; Chol 47mg; Iron 2mg; Sodium 237mg; Calc 36mg

 SIMPLE SWAP ◀ **Chicken tenders can be used in place of the turkey.**

Turkey Jambalaya

HANDS-ON TIME: 20 min. **TOTAL TIME:** 30 min.

 PREP TIP *Instead of buying chopped vegetables in the produce department, you can use frozen chopped peppers and onions, such as Birds Eye brand, and sauté these with the garlic in step 1.*

1 tablespoon olive oil

1½ cups prechopped onion

1 teaspoon bottled minced garlic

1 cup prechopped green bell pepper

1 cup prechopped red bell pepper

2½ teaspoons paprika

½ teaspoon salt

½ teaspoon dried oregano

½ teaspoon ground red pepper

½ teaspoon freshly ground black pepper

1 cup uncooked long-grain rice

2 cups fat-free, lower-sodium chicken broth

1 (14.5-ounce) can diced tomatoes, undrained

2 cups shredded cooked turkey

6 ounces andouille sausage, chopped

2 tablespoons sliced green onions

1 **Heat a large Dutch oven** over medium-high heat. Add oil to pan; swirl to coat. Add onion and garlic; sauté 6 minutes or until lightly browned.

2 **Stir in bell peppers and next 5 ingredients** (through black pepper); sauté 1 minute. Add rice; sauté 1 minute.

3 **Stir in broth and tomatoes;** bring to a boil. Cover, reduce heat, and simmer 15 minutes. Add turkey and sausage; cover and cook 5 minutes. Sprinkle with green onions. Serves 8 (serving size: 1 cup)

Calories 249; Fat 7.6g (sat 2.4g, mono 3.4g, poly 1.3g); Protein 17.3g; Carb 27.4g; Fiber 2.7g; Chol 42mg; Iron 2.7mg; Sodium 523mg; Calc 37mg

 SERVE WITH *This wonderfully spicy dish goes well with sweet corn-on-the-cob and fresh bread.*

Barley-Sausage Skillet

HANDS-ON TIME: 16 min. **TOTAL TIME:** 16 min.

PREP TIP *Madeira is a slightly sweet, fortified Portuguese wine. Substitute sherry or fruity white wine, if that's what you have on hand.*

1 (14-ounce) can fat-free, lower-sodium chicken broth
1 cup quick-cooking barley
Cooking spray
8 ounces hot turkey Italian sausage
1 teaspoon olive oil
1 cup prechopped onion

½ cup prechopped red bell pepper
1 (8-ounce) package presliced mushrooms
2 teaspoons bottled minced garlic
2 tablespoons Madeira wine
¼ cup thinly sliced fresh basil
⅛ teaspoon black pepper

1 **Place broth in a small saucepan;** bring to a boil. Add barley to pan. Cover, reduce heat, and simmer 10 minutes or until liquid is absorbed.

2 **While barley cooks,** heat a large nonstick skillet over medium-high heat. Coat pan with cooking spray. Remove casings from sausage. Add sausage to pan; cook 3 minutes, stirring to crumble. Transfer to a bowl.

3 **Heat oil in pan** over medium-high heat. Add onion, bell pepper, and mushrooms; sauté 4 minutes or until liquid evaporates. Add garlic; sauté 1 minute. Return sausage to pan. Stir in Madeira; sauté 2 minutes. Add barley; cook 1 minute or until thoroughly heated. Remove from heat; stir in basil and black pepper. Serves 4 (serving size: 1¼ cups)

Calories 337; Fat 8.1g (sat 3.7g, mono 2.6g, poly 1.6g); Protein 17.6g; Carb 49.1g; Fiber 9.6g; Chol 34mg; Iron 3mg; Sodium 537mg; Calc 49mg

SERVE WITH *Serve with broccoli sautéed with garlic and lemon, and warm corn bread.*

SERVE WITH

Serve with a wild rice mix, which you should start cooking before the cutlets.

Turkey Piccata

HANDS-ON TIME: 16 min. **TOTAL TIME:** 16 min.

 PREP TIP *Wine is used to deglaze the skillet, capturing the flavorful browned bits that remain after cooking the turkey.*

8 (3-ounce) turkey cutlets
¼ teaspoon salt
¼ teaspoon freshly ground black pepper
1 tablespoon olive oil, divided
2 tablespoons unsalted butter, divided
¼ cup chopped shallots
1 tablespoon sliced fresh garlic
¾ cup dry white wine
½ cup unsalted chicken stock
1 teaspoon all-purpose flour
2 tablespoons fresh lemon juice
1½ tablespoons capers, drained
2 tablespoons chopped fresh flat-leaf parsley

1 **Sprinkle turkey** evenly with salt and pepper. Heat a large skillet over medium-high heat. Add 1½ teaspoons oil to pan; swirl to coat. Add 4 cutlets to pan, and cook 2 minutes on each side or until done. Remove cutlets from pan; keep warm. Repeat procedure with remaining oil and cutlets.

2 **Add 1 tablespoon butter to pan.** Add shallots and garlic; sauté 1 minute. Increase heat to high. Add wine; bring to a boil, and cook 2 minutes, scraping pan to loosen browned bits.

3 **Combine chicken stock** and flour, stirring with a whisk. Add stock mixture to pan, and bring to a boil. Cook 5 minutes or until liquid is reduced by half. Remove from heat; stir in remaining 1 tablespoon butter, juice, and capers. Pour sauce over cutlets; sprinkle with parsley. Serves 4 (serving size: 2 cutlets and 2 tablespoons sauce)

Calories 298; Fat 10g (sat 4.1g, mono 4g, poly 0.6g); Protein 43.3g; Carb 4.5g; Fiber 0.6g; Chol 83mg; Iron 2.7mg; Sodium 414mg; Calc 19mg

 SIMPLE SWAP Chicken cutlets can be substituted for turkey cutlets. Make your own by cutting 4 chicken breasts in half horizontally.

Superfast Salisbury Steak

HANDS-ON TIME: 5 min. **TOTAL TIME:** 30 min.

PREP TIP *We used a blend of two kinds of ground meats for the patties. The turkey breast brings the total fat down, while the ground round adds moistness and flavor.*

¾ pound ground turkey breast

¾ pound ground round

⅓ cup dry breadcrumbs

2 large egg whites

¾ cup water

3 tablespoons unsalted tomato paste

2 tablespoons Madeira wine or dry sherry

1½ teaspoons Worcestershire sauce

¼ teaspoon freshly ground black pepper

1 (10½-ounce) can condensed French onion soup (such as Campbell's)

1 Combine first 4 ingredients. Divide meat mixture into 6 equal portions, shaping each into a ½-inch-thick patty.

2 Heat a large nonstick skillet over medium-high heat. Add patties; cook 6 minutes or until browned, turning after 3 minutes. Remove patties from pan; keep warm.

3 Add ¾ cup water and remaining ingredients to skillet; stir. Bring to a boil; add patties. Cover, reduce heat, and simmer 10 minutes. Uncover and cook until wine mixture is reduced to ¾ cup (about 9 minutes). Serves 6 (serving size: 1 patty and 2 tablespoons sauce)

Calories 210; Fat 5.9g (sat 2g, mono 1.9g, poly 0.8g); Protein 27.4g; Carb 10g; Fiber 0.9g; Chol 64mg; Iron 2.4mg; Sodium 504mg; Calc 38mg

SIMPLE SWAP Chicken broth can be used in place of the wine, if preferred.

Curried Beef

HANDS-ON TIME: 10 min. **TOTAL TIME:** 19 min.

 PREP TIP *Start step 2 as soon as you put the water for the rice on to boil—no need to wait until the water boils before starting the steak.*

1 (3½-ounce) bag boil-in-bag long-grain rice
1 (1-pound) flank steak, trimmed
Cooking spray
½ cup (1-inch) sliced green onions
1 teaspoon bottled minced garlic

1 tablespoon ground coriander
1 teaspoon ground cumin
½ teaspoon salt
¼ teaspoon ground turmeric
1 (14.5-ounce) can diced tomatoes, drained

1 **Prepare rice** according to package directions.

2 **While rice cooks,** cut steak diagonally across the grain into thin slices. Heat a large nonstick skillet over medium-high heat. Coat pan with cooking spray. Add onions and garlic; sauté 2 minutes. Add coriander, cumin, salt, and turmeric; sauté 1 minute.

3 **Add steak;** sauté 6 minutes or until done. Add tomatoes, and reduce heat to low. Cook 3 minutes or until thoroughly heated. Serve over rice. Serves 4 (serving size: 1 cup beef mixture and ½ cup rice)

Calories 394; Fat 12g (sat 5g, mono 4.7g, poly 0.5g); Protein 34.3g; Carb 34.4g; Fiber 2.6g; Chol 76mg; Iron 3.6mg; Sodium 490mg; Calc 40mg

 SERVE WITH *Pair this with Glazed Baby Carrots (page 203). Start cooking the carrots during step 2 of the beef recipe.*

SERVE WITH

Serve with Roasted Brussels Sprouts (page 201), cooking the Brussels sprouts while the beef cooks.

Beef Stroganoff

HANDS-ON TIME: 8 min. **TOTAL TIME:** 25 min.

 PREP TIP *We use beef broth to deglaze the skillet, adding to the richness of the sauce.*

6½ cups water, divided
4 ounces uncooked egg noodles
1 (1-pound) flank steak, trimmed
Cooking spray
1 cup prechopped onion
½ teaspoon freshly ground black pepper
½ teaspoon kosher salt
¼ teaspoon hot paprika
1 (6-ounce) package presliced exotic mushroom blend
1 cup lower-sodium beef broth, divided
5 teaspoons all-purpose flour
⅓ cup fat-free sour cream
3 tablespoons thinly sliced green onions
1 tablespoon butter
2 tablespoons chopped fresh flat-leaf parsley

 Bring 6 cups water to a boil in a large saucepan. Add noodles; cook 5 minutes or until al dente. Drain.

While noodles cook, cut beef across the grain into ¼-inch-wide strips; cut strips into 2-inch pieces. Heat a large skillet over medium-high heat. Coat pan with cooking spray. Add beef to pan; sauté 4 minutes or until browned. Remove beef from pan. Add 1 cup onion, black pepper, salt, paprika, and mushrooms to pan; sauté 4 minutes or until tender. Reduce heat to medium.

 Combine ¼ cup beef broth and flour in a small bowl, stirring with a whisk. Add broth mixture, beef, remaining ¾ cup broth, and ½ cup water to pan, scraping pan to loosen browned bits. Cover and cook 8 minutes or until sauce thickens. Remove from heat; stir in sour cream, green onions, and butter. Serve beef mixture over egg noodles; sprinkle with parsley. Serves 4 (serving size: 1 cup beef mixture and 1 cup noodles)

Calories 357; Fat 11.1g (sat 4.7g, mono 3g, poly 0.4g); Protein 31.9g; Carb 31.9g; Fiber 2.5g; Chol 80mg; Iron 3.4mg; Sodium 457mg; Calc 83mg

 SIMPLE SWAP Sliced button mushrooms can be used in place of the mushroom blend.

Mini Meat Loaves

HANDS-ON TIME: 7 min. **TOTAL TIME:** 32 min.

PREP TIP *Cooking mini meat loaves in single-serving portions cuts the usual cooking time in half. Be sure to gently shape the mixture into loaves—overworking the mixture will make them tough.*

- 6 tablespoons ketchup
- 1 tablespoon Dijon mustard
- 1 pound ground sirloin
- ³/₄ cup finely chopped onion
- ¹/₄ cup seasoned breadcrumbs
- ¹/₈ teaspoon salt
- ¹/₂ teaspoon dried oregano
- ¹/₈ teaspoon black pepper
- 1 large egg, lightly beaten
- Cooking spray

1 **Preheat** oven to 400°.

2 **Combine ketchup and mustard,** stirring well with a whisk. Reserve 2 tablespoons ketchup mixture. Gently combine remaining ketchup mixture, beef, and next 6 ingredients (through egg) in a large bowl, stirring to combine.

3 **Divide beef mixture** into 4 equal portions. Shape each portion into a 4 x 2¹/₂-inch loaf; place loaves on a jelly-roll pan coated with cooking spray. Spread about 2 teaspoons reserved ketchup mixture evenly over each loaf. Bake at 400° for 25 minutes or until done. Serves 4 (serving size: 1 loaf)

Calories 246; Fat 7.9g (sat 2.8g, mono 3.2g, poly 0.4g); Protein 27.4g; Carb 13.5g; Fiber 0.9g; Chol 120mg; Iron 2.7mg; Sodium 597mg; Calc 31mg

SERVE WITH *Serve with green beans and mashed potatoes. Refrigerated mashed potatoes take only a few minutes to heat.*

Sirloin Steaks *with* Mushroom Sauce (pictured on page 5)

HANDS-ON TIME: 5 min. **TOTAL TIME:** 12 min.

PREP TIP

Starting the skillet at medium-high heat allows the steaks to sear quickly on the outside. Then reduce heat to medium to allow the steaks to cook to the desired doneness.

4 **(4-ounce) boneless sirloin steaks, trimmed (about 1 inch thick)**
$^3/_8$ **teaspoon freshly ground black pepper, divided**
$^1/_4$ **teaspoon salt, divided**
1 **tablespoon olive oil**
1 **(8-ounce) package sliced cremini mushrooms**
$^1/_2$ **cup dry red wine**
$^1/_2$ **cup water**
2 **teaspoons all-purpose flour**

Sprinkle steaks evenly with $^1/_4$ teaspoon pepper and $^1/_8$ teaspoon salt. Heat oil in a large nonstick skillet over medium-high heat. Reduce heat to medium. Add steaks to pan; cook 2 minutes on each side or until desired degree of doneness. Remove from pan; keep warm.

Add mushrooms to pan; cook 5 minutes or until tender and beginning to brown, stirring frequently.

Combine wine, $^1/_2$ cup water, flour, $^1/_8$ teaspoon pepper, and $^1/_8$ teaspoon salt; stir well with a whisk. Add wine mixture to pan; bring to a boil. Cook 2 minutes or until thick; stir constantly. Remove from heat. Serves 4 (serving size: 1 steak and $^1/_4$ cup sauce)

Calories 215; Fat 8.23g (sat 2.2g, mono 4.9g, poly 0.6g); Protein 25.8g; Carb 4.2g; Fiber 0.4g; Chol 67mg; Iron 2.2mg; Sodium 213mg; Calc 38mg

SERVE WITH

These easy skillet-cooked steaks are accented with a rich wine and mushroom sauce for an easy weeknight dinner. Serve with quick-cooking wild rice and a mixed green salad.

Tex-Mex Nachos

HANDS-ON TIME: 15 min. **TOTAL TIME:** 15 min.

 PREP TIP *While the meat cooks, open the cans of beans and corn and measure the remaining ingredients so that they'll be ready to add to the skillet.*

3/4 pound ground round

1/4 cup sliced green onions

3/4 cup taco sauce

1/4 teaspoon garlic powder

1/8 teaspoon pepper

1 (15-ounce) can kidney beans, drained

1 (8³/4-ounce) can no-salt-added whole-kernel corn, drained

2 ounces fat-free baked tortilla chips (about 2 cups or about 18 chips)

1 (8-ounce) package shredded iceberg lettuce (about 3 cups)

1 cup prechopped tomato

4 ounces preshredded reduced-fat sharp cheddar or Monterey Jack cheese (about 1 cup)

1/2 cup bottled salsa

1/2 cup fat-free sour cream

1 **Cook meat and green onions** in a large nonstick skillet over medium-high heat until browned, stirring to crumble. Drain well, and return meat mixture to pan.

2 **Stir in taco sauce,** garlic powder, pepper, beans, and corn; cook until thoroughly heated.

3 **Spoon 1 cup meat mixture** over 1/2 cup chips, and top with 3/4 cup lettuce, 1/4 cup tomato, 1/4 cup cheese, 2 tablespoons salsa, and 2 tablespoons sour cream. Repeat three times with remaining ingredients. Serves 4

Calories 504; Fat 12.5g (sat 5.3g, mono 3.9g, poly 0.7g); Protein 39g; Carb 57.4g; Fiber 5.1g; Chol 73mg; Iron 4.5mg; Sodium 804mg; Calc 302mg

 SIMPLE SWAP Ground turkey and chicken are options instead of beef. Kick up the flavor with sliced jalapeño peppers.

Pork Chops *with* Country Gravy *and* Mashed Potatoes

HANDS-ON TIME: 5 min. **TOTAL TIME:** 18 min.

PREP TIP *These delicious pork chops are browned in butter, and then simmered in a homemade country gravy until done, which keeps the chops moist and juicy.*

- **³/₄ teaspoon salt, divided**
- **4 (4-ounce) boneless center-cut loin pork chops (about 1 inch thick)**
- **1 teaspoon butter**
- **1¹/₃ cups 1% low-fat milk**
- **3 tablespoons all-purpose flour**

- **¹/₄ teaspoon poultry seasoning**
- **¹/₄ teaspoon black pepper**
- **1 (20-ounce) package refrigerated mashed potatoes (such as Simply Potatoes)**
- **Chopped fresh parsley (optional)**

1 **Heat** a large nonstick skillet over medium-high heat. Sprinkle ¹/₄ teaspoon salt evenly over both sides of pork. Add butter to pan, stirring until melted. Add pork, and cook 3 minutes on each side. Remove pork from pan; keep warm.

2 **Combine milk and flour,** stirring with a whisk. Add milk mixture to pan, stirring with a whisk. Stir in remaining ¹/₂ teaspoon salt, poultry seasoning, and black pepper. Return pork to pan. Cover; reduce heat, and simmer 7 minutes or until gravy is thick and pork is done.

3 **While pork cooks,** prepare potatoes according to package directions. Serve with pork. Garnish with parsley, if desired. Serves 4 (serving size: 1 pork chop, ²/₃ cup potatoes, and ¹/₄ cup gravy)

Calories 322; Fat 10.5g (sat 3.7g, mono 3.9g, poly 0.5g); Protein 26.7g; Carb 29g; Fiber 2.2g; Chol 65mg; Iron 1mg; Sodium 708mg; Calc 125mg

SERVE WITH *Serve with frozen mixed vegetables: Simply steam them while the meat and potatoes cook. The five-ingredient gravy also goes well over pan-sautéed or oven-fried chicken or an open-faced turkey sandwich.*

SERVE WITH *Serve the chops with whipped sweet potatoes.*

58

Pork Chops Marsala

HANDS-ON TIME: 7 min. **TOTAL TIME:** 18 min.

 PREP TIP *Save time in the kitchen by purchasing a bottle of minced garlic and presliced mushrooms.*

- 6 tablespoons all-purpose flour, divided
- 4 (4-ounce) boneless center-cut loin pork chops (about ½ inch thick)
- Cooking spray
- ⅓ cup minced shallots (about 2)
- 2 teaspoons bottled minced garlic
- 1 (8-ounce) package presliced mushrooms
- 2 teaspoons chopped fresh thyme
- 1 cup fat-free, lower-sodium chicken broth
- ¼ cup Marsala wine or dry sherry
- ¼ teaspoon salt
- ¼ teaspoon freshly ground black pepper

 **1** **Heat a large** nonstick skillet over medium-high heat. Place ¼ cup flour in a shallow dish. Dredge pork in flour. Coat pan with cooking spray. Add pork to pan; cook 4 minutes on each side or until browned. Remove pork from pan.

2 **Add shallots, garlic,** and mushrooms to pan; sauté 3 minutes or until moisture evaporates. Add 2 tablespoons flour and thyme to pan; cook 1 minute, stirring well. Combine broth and Marsala, stirring until smooth. Gradually add broth mixture to pan, stirring constantly with a whisk; bring to a boil. Reduce heat, and simmer 2 minutes or until sauce thickens.

 3 **Return pork to pan;** cook 2 minutes or until pork loses its pink color, turning to coat. Sprinkle with salt and pepper. Serves 4 (serving size: 1 pork chop and ½ cup sauce)

Calories 242; Fat 6.8g (sat 2.5g, mono 2.9g, poly 0.6g); Protein 27g; Carb 15.4g; Fiber 1.1g; Chol 67mg; Iron 2.1mg; Sodium 299mg; Calc 44mg

 SIMPLE SWAP Skinless, boneless chicken breast halves, pounded ½-inch thick, can be used in place of the pork.

+ SERVE WITH **Round out the meal with steamed green beans or a spinach salad.**

Smothered Pork Chops *with* Onions *and* Cheddar Grits

HANDS-ON TIME: 15 min. **TOTAL TIME:** 15 min.

 PREP TIP *Cook the grits in the microwave, if you'd like. Just be sure to use a large enough bowl so they don't boil over.*

2²/₃ cups water

2/₃ cup uncooked quick-cooking grits

1 ounce preshredded sharp cheddar cheese (about ¼ cup)

½ teaspoon salt, divided

⅛ teaspoon garlic powder

Dash of ground red pepper

4 (4-ounce) boneless center-cut loin pork chops, trimmed

½ teaspoon garlic powder

⅛ teaspoon freshly ground black pepper

3 tablespoons all-purpose flour

2 teaspoons butter

1 cup prechopped onion

½ cup fat-free, lower-sodium chicken broth

¼ cup water

Fresh thyme (optional)

1 **Bring 2²/₃ cups water to a boil;** stir in grits. Reduce heat, and cook 5 minutes, stirring frequently. Remove from heat. Stir in cheese, ¼ teaspoon salt, ⅛ teaspoon garlic powder, and red pepper.

2 **While grits cook,** sprinkle pork with remaining ¼ teaspoon salt, ½ teaspoon garlic powder, and black pepper. Dredge in flour.

3 **Melt butter** in a large nonstick skillet over medium-high heat. Add pork and onion; sauté 6 minutes, turning pork over after 3 minutes. Add broth and ¼ cup water; bring to a boil. Cover, reduce heat, and simmer 4 minutes. Serve with grits. Garnish with thyme, if desired. Serves 4 (serving size: 1 pork chop and ½ cup grits)

Calories 394; Fat 17.6g (sat 7.3g, mono 6.3g, poly 1.5g); Protein 27.8g; Carb 29.3g; Fiber 1.4g; Chol 83mg; Iron 1.9mg; Sodium 427mg; Calc 82mg

 SIMPLE SWAP **Serve whole grain brown rice in place of the cheese grits, if you prefer. Use two 8.8-ounce packages precooked whole grain brown rice, and heat according to package directions.**

Honey- *and* Spice- Glazed Pork Chops

HANDS-ON TIME: 5 min. **TOTAL TIME:** 15 min.

 PREP TIP *Measure the honey and seasonings while the pork cooks, and you'll keep the recipe to 15 minutes total.*

Cooking spray

4 (4-ounce) boneless center-cut loin pork chops (about $\frac{1}{2}$ inch thick)

$\frac{1}{2}$ teaspoon salt

$\frac{1}{4}$ teaspoon freshly ground black pepper

$\frac{1}{4}$ cup honey

2 tablespoons Dijon mustard

$\frac{1}{2}$ teaspoon ground ginger

$\frac{1}{4}$ teaspoon ground cinnamon

$\frac{1}{8}$ teaspoon ground cloves

1 tablespoon chopped fresh parsley (optional)

1 **Heat a large nonstick** skillet over medium-high heat. Coat pan with cooking spray. Sprinkle pork with salt and pepper. Add pork to pan; cook 2 minutes on each side or until browned.

2 **While pork cooks,** combine honey and next 4 ingredients (through cloves) in a bowl.

3 **Reduce heat to medium-low,** and add honey mixture to pork. Cook 10 minutes or until done, turning pork once. Garnish with parsley, if desired. Serves 4 (serving size: 1 pork chop and 1 tablespoon glaze)

Calories 321; Fat 12.1g (sat 4.1g, mono 5.5g, poly 0.9g); Protein 34g; Carb 18.7g; Fiber 0.3g; Chol 92mg; Iron 1.3mg; Sodium 557mg; Calc 50mg

 SIMPLE SWAP Chicken or turkey cutlets can be used in place of the pork chops.

Breaded Pork Cutlets

HANDS-ON TIME: 10 min. **TOTAL TIME:** 15 min.

PREP TIP

Breaded pork cutlets can get soggy while waiting for the pan to heat. Once breaded, place them on a wire rack that's resting over a baking sheet.

- 2 (1-ounce) slices white bread
- ¾ teaspoon kosher salt
- ½ teaspoon freshly ground black pepper
- ½ teaspoon dried rubbed sage
- ½ teaspoon dried thyme
- 8 (2-ounce) boneless pork chops (¼ inch thick)

- 1.1 ounces all-purpose flour (about ¼ cup)
- 3 large egg whites, lightly beaten
- 2 teaspoons canola oil
- Cooking spray
- 4 lemon wedges

1 **Place bread slices** in a food processor; pulse 10 times or until coarse crumbs measure 1 cup. Place breadcrumbs in a shallow dish.

2 **Combine salt, pepper,** sage, and thyme; sprinkle over both sides of pork. Place flour in a shallow dish; place egg whites in another shallow dish. Dredge pork in flour, dip in egg whites, and dredge in breadcrumbs.

3 **Heat a large nonstick** skillet over medium-high heat. Add oil to pan; swirl to coat. Add pork, and cook 2½ minutes or until lightly browned. Lightly coat surface of chops with cooking spray; turn chops over. Cook 2½ minutes or until done. Serve with lemon wedges. Serves 4 (serving size: 2 pork chops and 1 lemon wedge)

Calories 245; Fat 8g (sat 2.2g, mono 2.9g, poly 1.8g); Protein 28.4g; Carb 13g; Fiber 0.8g; Chol 70mg; Iron 1.9mg; Sodium 502mg; Calc 33mg

Maple- *and* Balsamic- Glazed Pork Medallions

HANDS-ON TIME: 8 min. **TOTAL TIME:** 14 min.

 PREP TIP *Pounding the pork helps shorten cooking time, leaving it tender and juicy.*

¼ cup maple syrup

3 tablespoons balsamic vinegar

2 teaspoons Dijon mustard

1 (1-pound) pork tenderloin, trimmed

2 teaspoons olive oil

½ teaspoon salt

¼ teaspoon freshly ground black pepper

 1 **Combine syrup and vinegar** in a small saucepan; bring to a boil. Cook until reduced to ⅓ cup (about 3 minutes), stirring occasionally. Remove from heat; stir in mustard.

 2 **While syrup cooks,** cut pork crosswise into 8 pieces. Place each pork piece between 2 sheets of heavy-duty plastic wrap; pound to ¼-inch thickness using a meat mallet or small heavy skillet.

 3 **Heat a large nonstick** skillet over medium-high heat. Add oil to pan; swirl to coat. Sprinkle pork evenly with salt and pepper. Add pork to pan; cook 3 minutes on each side. Add vinegar mixture; cook 1 minute or until desired degree of doneness, turning pork to coat. Place 2 pork medallions on each of 4 plates; drizzle about 1 tablespoon syrup mixture over each serving. Serves 4

Calories 214; Fat 6.4g (sat 1.7g, mono 3.3g, poly 0.7g); Protein 22.7g; Carb 15.3g; Fiber 0.1g; Chol 63mg; Iron 1.5mg; Sodium 409mg; Calc 22mg

 SERVE WITH *Serve with heat-and-serve brown rice and sautéed broccoli rabe.*

Ham *and* Cheese Hash Browns

HANDS-ON TIME: 9 min. **TOTAL TIME:** 14 min.

PREP TIP *A great use for leftover ham, this recipe resembles a skillet potato hash. The surprise is that it's more easily prepared in the microwave. No need to thaw the hash brown potatoes; they go straight from the freezer into the microwave.*

3 cups frozen hash brown potatoes with onions and peppers (such as Ore-Ida Potatoes O'Brien)

1/3 cup fat-free, lower-sodium chicken broth

1/2 cup drained canned quartered artichoke hearts, chopped

1/4 cup chopped green onions

1/8 teaspoon freshly ground black pepper

3 ounces 33%-less-sodium ham, cut into bite-sized pieces

2 ounces preshredded Monterey Jack cheese (about 1/2 cup)

1 **Combine potatoes** and chicken broth in a 1-quart microwave-safe casserole. Cover with lid, and microwave at HIGH 12 minutes, stirring after 6 minutes.

2 **Stir in artichoke hearts,** green onions, black pepper, and ham. Sprinkle with cheese.

3 **Microwave, uncovered,** at HIGH 1 minute. Serves 2 (serving size: 1 3/4 cups)

Calories 378; Fat 12.5g (sat 6.2g, mono 2.7g, poly 1.4g); Protein 20g; Carb 41.8g; Fiber 6.1g; Chol 55mg; Iron 1.3mg; Sodium 591mg; Calc 204mg

SERVE WITH *Pair this with fresh fruit or a green salad for an effortless dinner.*

Ham- *and* Swiss-Loaded Potatoes

HANDS-ON TIME: 5 min. **TOTAL TIME:** 29 min.

PREP TIP *Using a microwave to cook the potatoes first saves more than an hour of baking time. Use tangy cheddar instead of Swiss, if you like.*

4 **baking potatoes (about 1½ pounds)**

1 **cup diced 33%-less-sodium ham (about 6 ounces)**

4 **ounces shredded Swiss cheese, divided (about 1 cup)**

½ **cup thinly sliced green onions, divided**

½ **cup fat-free sour cream**

¼ **teaspoon freshly ground black pepper**

Chopped fresh chives (optional)

1 **Pierce potatoes with a fork;** arrange in a circle on paper towels in microwave oven. Microwave at HIGH 16 minutes or until done, rearranging potatoes after 8 minutes. Let stand 5 minutes.

2 **Preheat broiler.** Cut each potato in half lengthwise; scoop out pulp, leaving a ¼-inch-thick shell.

3 **Combine potato pulp,** ham, ½ cup cheese, ⅓ cup green onions, sour cream, and pepper; spoon into potato shells. Combine ½ cup cheese and remaining green onions; sprinkle over potatoes. Place potatoes on a baking sheet; broil 4 minutes or until golden. Garnish with chives, if desired. Serves 4 (serving size: 2 potato halves)

Calories 376; Fat 11g (sat 6.2g, mono 3.5g, poly 0.7g); Protein 20.1g; Carb 47.9g; Fiber 3.4g; Chol 51mg; Iron 2.9mg; Sodium 540mg; Calc 359mg

SERVE WITH *Piled high with ham, cheese, and sour cream, this filling dish makes for an easy weeknight supper when paired with a salad.*

Southern-Style Shrimp,
page 93

3

seafood »

Fast-cooking seafood offers a light option, ideal for any night of the week. Add some flavorful herbs, and dinner's on the table in a jiffy.

Cajun Catfish

HANDS-ON TIME: 2 min. **TOTAL TIME:** 12 min.

PREP TIP *Start by preheating the broiler so that it'll be ready when you are. The fish can also be grilled, or you can wrap the fillets in foil, and bake for 15 minutes at 400°.*

4 (4-ounce) farm-raised catfish fillets
1 tablespoon fresh lemon juice

4 teaspoons Cajun seasoning
Cooking spray

1 Preheat broiler.

2 Brush both sides of fillets with lemon juice, and sprinkle with Cajun seasoning.

3 Place fish on a broiler pan coated with cooking spray, and broil 5 minutes on each side until fish flakes easily when tested with a fork or until desired degree of doneness. Serves 4 (serving size: 1 fillet)

Calories 140; Fat 5.1g (sat 1.2g, mono 1.8g, poly 1.3g); Protein 20.1g; Carb 1.5g; Fiber 0.3g; Chol 66mg; Iron 1.6mg; Sodium 219mg; Calc 56mg

SERVE WITH *Serve with sautéed corn and tomatoes: Sauté 2 cups frozen corn and 1 cup quartered cherry tomatoes in 1 teaspoon olive oil for 3 minutes or until tender. Add 1 tablespoon sherry vinegar, 2 teaspoons minced fresh thyme, and ½ teaspoon freshly ground pepper.*

Crisp-Crusted Catfish

HANDS-ON TIME: 5 min. **TOTAL TIME:** 28 min.

 PREP TIP *Once the fish is in the oven, you'll have time to prepare Easy Stovetop Mac and Cheese (page 131).*

2 tablespoons light ranch dressing

2 large egg whites

6 tablespoons yellow cornmeal

1 ounce (¼ cup) grated fresh Parmesan cheese

2 tablespoons all-purpose flour

¼ teaspoon ground red pepper

⅛ teaspoon salt

4 (6-ounce) farm-raised catfish fillets

Cooking spray

4 lemon wedges

1 **Preheat** oven to 425°.

2 **Combine dressing and egg whites in a small bowl;** stir well with a whisk. Combine cornmeal, cheese, flour, pepper, and salt in a shallow dish. Dip fish in egg white mixture; dredge in cornmeal mixture.

3 **Place fish on a baking sheet coated with cooking spray;** bake at 425° for 12 minutes on each side or until lightly browned and fish flakes easily when tested with a fork or until desired degree of doneness. Serve with lemon wedges. Serves 4 (serving size: 1 fillet and 1 lemon wedge)

Calories 313; Fat 9.1g (sat 2.8g, mono 3.6g, poly 3.3g); Protein 32.9g; Carb 14.3g; Fiber 1.1g; Chol 87mg; Iron 1.2mg; Sodium 348mg; Calc 101mg

 SERVE WITH *Serve with Lemon Pepper Veggies (page 198) for a Southern meal without the grease. If you have leftovers, the fish goes well in tacos for another meal.*

SERVE
WITH

Serve with quick-to-prepare Cilantro-Chipotle Rice (page 215).

Baja Fish Tacos

HANDS-ON TIME: 15 min. **TOTAL TIME:** 15 min.

 PREP TIP *If you prefer your slaw with peppery bite, add chopped green chiles to the cabbage mix.*

2 tablespoons taco seasoning
1 tablespoon fresh lime juice
1 tablespoon orange juice
1 pound mahimahi or other firm white fish fillets, cut into bite-sized pieces
1 tablespoon canola oil
2 cups presliced green cabbage
½ cup prechopped purple onion
½ cup chopped green onions
½ cup reduced-fat sour cream
8 (6-inch) corn tortillas
8 lime wedges
Fresh cilantro (optional)

 Combine first 3 ingredients in a medium bowl. Add fish; toss to coat.

 Heat a large nonstick skillet over medium-high heat. Add oil to pan; swirl to coat. Add fish; sauté 5 minutes or until fish flakes easily when tested with a fork or until desired degree of doneness.

 While fish cooks, combine cabbage, onions, and sour cream in a medium bowl. Warm tortillas according to package directions. Spoon about ¼ cup cabbage mixture down center of each tortilla. Divide fish evenly among tortillas; fold in half. Serve with lime wedges. Garnish with cilantro, if desired. Serves 4 (serving size: 2 fish tacos and 2 lime wedges)

Calories 327; Fat 9.4g (sat 3.3g, mono 1.3g, poly 2.8g); Protein 26g; Carb 35.8g; Fiber 4.6g; Chol 98mg; Iron 2.4mg; Sodium 624mg; Calc 182mg

 SIMPLE SWAP **Tilapia imparts a mild fish flavor when used in these tacos.**

Parmesan- *and* Herb-Baked Flounder

HANDS-ON TIME: 5 min. **TOTAL TIME:** 15 min.

PREP TIP *Mayonnaise helps the breadcrumbs adhere to the fish. While the fish bakes, prepare quick-cooking wild rice, which can be heated in just five minutes.*

4 (6-ounce) flounder fillets
Cooking spray
1½ ounces (about ⅓ cup) grated fresh Parmesan cheese
¼ cup canola mayonnaise
2 tablespoons minced green onions

¼ cup dry breadcrumbs
1 teaspoon dried basil
1 teaspoon dried oregano
⅛ teaspoon salt
¼ teaspoon black pepper
8 lemon wedges

1 **Preheat** oven to 400°. Place fish on a foil-lined baking sheet coated with cooking spray. Combine cheese, mayonnaise, and onions; spread evenly over fish.

2 **Combine breadcrumbs and next 4 ingredients** (through pepper); sprinkle evenly over fish. Lightly coat fish with cooking spray.

3 **Bake at 400°** for 10 minutes or until fish flakes easily when tested with a fork or until desired degree of doneness. Serve with lemon wedges. Serves 4 (serving size: 1 fillet and 2 lemon wedges)

Calories 241; Fat 5.5g (sat 1.9g, mono 1.1g, poly 0.7g); Protein 35.9g; Carb 10g; Fiber 0.7g; Chol 87mg; Iron 1.6mg; Sodium 534mg; Calc 157mg

SERVE WITH *Serve with quick-cooking wild rice, or on a hoagie roll with lettuce and tomato.*

Beer-Battered Fish

HANDS-ON TIME: 8 min. **TOTAL TIME:** 24 min.

 PREP TIP *You can use either dry breadcrumbs or panko (Japanese breadcrumbs)—both will make a crisp crust on the fish.*

1½ tablespoons canola oil

4.5 ounces all-purpose flour (about 1 cup)

½ teaspoon freshly ground black pepper

¼ teaspoon garlic salt

⅔ cup beer

2 large egg whites

2 cups dry breadcrumbs

½ cup chopped fresh parsley

1½ pounds grouper or other firm white fish fillets, cut into 4 x 1-inch strips

Cooking spray

Malt vinegar (optional)

 1 **Preheat oven to 450°.** Coat the bottom of a jelly-roll pan with oil. Combine flour, pepper, and garlic salt in a large bowl. Add beer; stir well. Beat egg whites with a mixer at high speed until stiff peaks form. Gently fold egg white mixture into flour mixture. Combine breadcrumbs and parsley in a shallow dish. Working with one fish strip at a time, dip in flour mixture; dredge in breadcrumb mixture. Repeat procedure with remaining strips, flour mixture, and breadcrumb mixture. Place on prepared pan. Lightly coat strips with cooking spray.

 2 **Bake at 450° for 15 minutes** or until fish flakes easily when tested with a fork or until desired degree of doneness. Remove from oven.

 3 **Preheat broiler.** Broil fish strips 1 minute or until lightly browned. Serve with malt vinegar, if desired. Serves 4 (serving size: 1 fish strip)

Calories 351; Fat 5.1g (sat 1g, mono 1.4g, poly 1.9g); Protein 39.1g; Carb 32.9g; Fiber 1.4g; Chol 63mg; Iron 4.4mg; Sodium 371mg; Calc 122mg

SERVE WITH *Serve with malt vinegar and garlic-baked fries for a healthier version of fish and chips.*

Easy Pesto Salmon

HANDS-ON TIME: 15 min. **TOTAL TIME:** 30 min.

 PREP TIP *The rice cooks quickly, so put the water on to boil midway through the bake time for the fish. By the time the water is hot and the rice simmers, the fish will be done.*

2 cups spinach leaves

½ cup basil leaves

¼ cup fat-free, lower-sodium chicken broth

1 tablespoon olive oil

¼ teaspoon salt

3 garlic cloves, peeled

Cooking spray

2 (6-ounce) salmon fillets, skinned

½ cup quick-cooking brown rice, uncooked

1 **Preheat** oven to 400°.

2 **Place first 6 ingredients** in a food processor or blender, and process until smooth. Spoon 3 tablespoons pesto into bottom of an 8-inch square baking dish coated with cooking spray. Top with salmon fillets, and spread with remaining pesto. Bake at 400° for 20 minutes or until fish flakes easily when tested with a fork or until desired degree of doneness.

3 **While fish bakes,** cook rice according to package directions, omitting salt and fat. Serve with fish. Serves 2 (serving size: 1 salmon fillet and ⅓ cup rice)

Calories 443; Fat 22.1g (sat 3.5g, mono 12g, poly 4.4g); Protein 38.7g; Carb 20.6g; Fiber 3.1g; Chol 111mg; Iron 3.2mg; Sodium 483mg; Calc 96mg

SIMPLE SWAP You can use ⅓ cup bottled pesto in place of the first 6 ingredients. Drain the extra oil from the top of the prepared pesto to save on calories and fat.

Salmon *with* Hoisin Glaze

HANDS-ON TIME: 3 min. **TOTAL TIME:** 17 min.

 PREP TIP *For quick cleanup, line the baking sheet with aluminum foil coated with cooking spray.*

2 tablespoons hoisin sauce
2 teaspoons lower-sodium soy sauce
1/2 teaspoon dark sesame oil
4 (6-ounce) skinless wild salmon fillets

Cooking spray
1 teaspoon sesame seeds
Lemon rind strips (optional)

1 **Preheat** oven to 400°.

2 **Combine first 3 ingredients** in a shallow dish. Add fish to dish, turning to coat. Marinate at room temperature 8 minutes, turning occasionally.

3 **Remove fish from marinade;** discard marinade. Place fish on a baking sheet coated with cooking spray. Sprinkle fish evenly with sesame seeds. Bake at 400° for 8 minutes or until fish flakes easily when tested with a fork or until desired degree of doneness. Garnish with rind, if desired.

Calories 255; Fat 11.7g (sat 2.7g, mono 4.8g, poly 2.8g); Protein 31.5g; Carb 3.9g; Fiber 0.3g; Chol 81mg; Iron 0.7mg; Sodium 285mg; Calc 26mg

 SERVE WITH *Enjoy with garlicky-spicy snow peas: Heat a nonstick skillet over medium-high heat. Add 1 teaspoon canola oil to pan; swirl to coat. Add 1 pound snow peas and 1/4 teaspoon salt; sauté 2 minutes. Stir in 2 teaspoons bottled minced garlic and 1/4 teaspoon crushed red pepper; sauté 1 minute. Stir in 1/4 teaspoon sugar; sauté 1 minute. Remove from heat; drizzle with 1/2 teaspoon dark sesame oil.*

Curry-Chutney Snapper

HANDS-ON TIME: 6 min. **TOTAL TIME:** 12 min.

 PREP TIP *Sherry or white wine are sophisticated substitutes for the chicken broth.*

2 tablespoons all-purpose flour
2 teaspoons curry powder
¼ teaspoon salt
4 (6-ounce) red snapper or mahimahi fillets
1 tablespoon butter
½ cup fat-free, lower-sodium chicken broth
¼ cup mango chutney
¼ teaspoon hot sauce
2 tablespoons minced fresh cilantro

1 **Combine first 3 ingredients** in a shallow dish. Dredge fish in flour mixture.

2 **Melt butter in a large nonstick skillet** over medium-high heat. Add fish; cook 3 minutes on each side or until fish flakes easily when tested with a fork or until desired degree of doneness. Remove from skillet; keep warm.

3 **Add broth, chutney, and hot sauce to skillet;** bring to a boil. Cook 1 minute, stirring constantly. Spoon sauce over fish; sprinkle with cilantro. Serves 4 (serving size: 1 fillet, 2 tablespoons sauce, and 1½ teaspoons cilantro.

Calories 257; Fat 5.3g (sat 1.1g, mono 1.8g, poly 1.7g); Protein 36.1g; Carb 14.4g; Fiber 0.5g; Chol 63mg; Iron 1.1mg; Sodium 386mg; Calc 69mg

 SERVE WITH *The curry flavor blends nicely with basmati rice with minted peas. To prepare this easy side dish, cook 2 (8.5-ounce) pouches ready-to-serve basmati rice according to package directions. Stir in 1 cup frozen green peas, thawed; ¼ cup chopped fresh parsley; and 1 tablespoon chopped fresh mint. Sprinkle with black pepper, if desired.*

Skillet Fillets *with* Cilantro Butter

HANDS-ON TIME: 7 min. **TOTAL TIME:** 10 min.

PREP TIP *The key to speed is to always look ahead in the recipe. Here, you can make the cilantro butter while the fish cooks.*

¼ teaspoon salt
¼ teaspoon ground cumin
⅛ teaspoon ground red pepper
4 (6-ounce) tilapia fillets
Cooking spray
1 lemon, quartered

2 tablespoons butter, softened
2 tablespoons finely chopped fresh cilantro
½ teaspoon grated lemon rind
¼ teaspoon paprika
⅛ teaspoon salt

1 Combine first 3 ingredients; sprinkle over both sides of fish.

2 Heat a large nonstick skillet over medium-high heat. Coat pan with cooking spray. Coat both sides of fish with cooking spray; place in pan. Cook 3 minutes on each side or until fish flakes easily when tested with a fork or until desired degree of doneness. Place fish on a serving platter; squeeze lemon quarters over fish.

3 While fish cooks, combine butter and remaining ingredients in a small bowl; stir until well blended. Serve with fish. Serves 4 (serving size: 1 fillet and about 2 teaspoons cilantro butter)

Calories 194; Fat 6.9g (sat 3.1g, mono 2.5g, poly 0.6g); Protein 30.5g; Carb 1.2g; Fiber 0.2g; Chol 88mg; Iron 0.7mg; Sodium 354mg; Calc 32mg

 SIMPLE SWAP Any mild white fish, such as cod, flounder, or orange roughy, would also be delicious in place of the tilapia.

SERVE WITH *Serve with coconut rice (substitute light coconut milk for some of the water to cook it). Round out this tilapia dish with a romaine lettuce salad tossed with lime dressing.*

Spicy Tilapia *with* Pineapple-Pepper Relish

HANDS-ON TIME: 15 min. **TOTAL TIME:** 15 min.

 PREP TIP *Fresh pineapple chunks, now widely available in supermarkets, speed the prep for this relish.*

2 teaspoons canola oil
1 teaspoon Cajun seasoning
¼ teaspoon kosher salt
¼ teaspoon ground red pepper
4 (6-ounce) tilapia fillets
1½ cups chopped fresh pineapple chunks
⅓ cup prechopped onion
⅓ cup chopped plum tomato
2 tablespoons rice vinegar
1 tablespoon chopped fresh cilantro
1 small jalapeño pepper, seeded and chopped
4 lime wedges

1 **Heat a large nonstick skillet** over medium-high heat. Add oil to pan; swirl to coat. Combine Cajun seasoning, salt, and red pepper in a small bowl. Sprinkle fish evenly with spice mixture.

2 **Add fish to pan,** and cook 2 minutes on each side or until fish flakes easily when tested with a fork or until desired degree of doneness.

3 **While fish cooks,** combine pineapple and next 5 ingredients (through jalapeño pepper) in a large bowl, stirring gently. Serve pineapple mixture with fish. Serve with lime wedges. Serves 4 (serving size: 1 fillet, about ½ cup relish, and 1 lime wedge)

Calories 228; Fat 5.5g (sat 1.2g, mono 2.2g, poly 1.4g); Protein 34.9g; Carb 11.2g; Fiber 1.5g; Chol 85mg; Iron 1.2mg; Sodium 328mg; Calc 29mg

 SIMPLE SWAP Mahimahi can be used for the tilapia. A small serrano pepper, which is about five times hotter than a jalapeño, can be used instead.

+ SERVE WITH

Serve with roasted potatoes and warm Italian whole-wheat bread. You can purchase refrigerated potato wedges, which can cook while you prepare the fish.

Tilapia in Mustard-Cream Sauce

HANDS-ON TIME: 12 min. **TOTAL TIME:** 12 min.

 PREP TIP *Gently remove the tender fillets from the pan after they're cooked to avoid breaking them apart.*

4 **(6-ounce) tilapia fillets**
½ **teaspoon chopped fresh thyme**
½ **teaspoon freshly ground black pepper**
¼ **teaspoon salt**
Cooking spray
¾ **cup fat-free, lower-sodium chicken broth**
1 **ounce baby portobello mushrooms, sliced**
2 **tablespoons whipping cream**
2 **tablespoons Dijon mustard**

1 **Sprinkle fish** with thyme, pepper, and salt.

2 **Heat a large nonstick skillet** over medium-high heat. Coat pan with cooking spray. Add fish; cook 1 minute on each side. Add broth, and bring to a boil. Cover, reduce heat, and simmer 5 minutes. Add mushrooms; cook, uncovered, 1 minute or until mushrooms are tender. Remove fish from pan; keep warm.

3 **Add cream and mustard to pan;** stir with a whisk until well combined. Cook 1 minute or until thoroughly heated. Serve sauce over fish. Serves 4 (serving size: 1 fillet and ¼ cup sauce)

Calories 184; Fat 4.6g (sat 2.1g, mono 1g, poly 0.4g); Protein 32.7g; Carb 1.2g; Fiber 0.6g; Chol 134mg; Iron 2.2mg; Sodium 536mg; Calc 40mg

 SIMPLE SWAP Orange roughy or chicken can be used instead of tilapia, and tomatoes or spinach can be substituted for mushrooms.

Pecan-Crusted Tilapia

HANDS-ON TIME: 6 min. **TOTAL TIME:** 18 min.

PREP TIP *Use two shallow dishes for step 1. They need to be large enough for a fillet to fit across the bottom of the dish.*

½ cup dry breadcrumbs
2 tablespoons finely chopped pecans
½ teaspoon salt
¼ teaspoon garlic powder
¼ teaspoon black pepper
½ cup low-fat buttermilk

½ teaspoon hot sauce
3 tablespoons all-purpose flour
4 (6-ounce) tilapia or snapper fillets
1 tablespoon canola oil, divided
4 lemon wedges

1 **Combine first 5 ingredients** in a shallow dish. Combine buttermilk and hot sauce in a medium bowl. Place flour in another shallow dish.

2 **Dredge 1 fillet in flour.** Dip in buttermilk mixture; dredge in breadcrumb mixture. Repeat procedure with remaining fillets, flour, buttermilk mixture, and breadcrumb mixture.

3 **Heat a large nonstick skillet** over medium-high heat. Add 1½ teaspoons oil to pan; swirl to coat. Add 2 fillets; cook 3 minutes on each side or until fish flakes easily when tested with a fork or until desired degree of doneness. Repeat procedure with remaining oil and fillets. Serve with lemon wedges. Serves 4 (serving size: 1 fillet and 1 lemon wedge)

Calories 302; Fat 9.1g (sat 1.1g, mono 3.9g, poly 2.6g); Protein 38.4g; Carb 14.2g; Fiber 0.9g; Chol 64mg; Iron 1.3mg; Sodium 530mg; Calc 98mg

SIMPLE SWAP **Mahimahi and halibut can be used instead of the tilapia. Add a taste of the tropics by using light coconut milk in place of buttermilk.**

Cajun Scallops

HANDS-ON TIME: 9 min. **TOTAL TIME:** 12 min.

 PREP TIP *The secret to getting a beautiful brown sear is to pat the scallops dry, sear them in a hot skillet, and move them only to turn them over.*

1 teaspoon olive oil
1 large red onion, thinly sliced and separated into rings
½ teaspoon Cajun seasoning
½ teaspoon freshly ground black pepper
1 teaspoon butter
1 teaspoon bottled minced garlic
¾ pound fresh scallops
1 to 2 teaspoons hot sauce

1 **Heat a cast-iron skillet** over high heat. Add oil to pan; swirl to coat. Add onion, Cajun seasoning, and pepper; sauté 3 minutes.

 2 **Add butter and garlic;** sauté 30 seconds.

 3 **Add scallops; cook 1 minute or until browned.** Sprinkle with hot sauce; turn. Cook 3 minutes or until desired degree of doneness. Serves 2 (serving size: about 5 ounces scallops)

Calories 225; Fat 5.7g (sat 1.7g, mono 2.3g, poly 0.8g); Protein 29.8g; Carb 12.5g; Fiber 1.8g; Chol 61mg; Iron 0.9mg; Sodium 589mg; Calc 65mg

 SERVE WITH *Cajun seasoning and hot sauce give the dish its heat, while sautéed red onion adds bite. Serve over rice for a hearty dinner, or on a bed of fresh baby spinach for a lighter meal.*

SERVE WITH *Serve this easy but impressive meal with a green salad, garlic bread, and a crisp white wine.*

Seared Scallops
with Lemon Orzo

HANDS-ON TIME: 7 min. **TOTAL TIME:** 19 min.

Look for dry-packed sea scallops at your local seafood market. Other scallops have been soaking in a liquid solution, which increases their weight and sodium content. Sear the scallops while the orzo cooks.

Cooking spray
- ½ **cup prechopped onion**
- 1 **cup uncooked orzo (rice-shaped pasta)**
- 1 **cup fat-free, lower-sodium chicken broth**
- ½ **cup dry white wine**
- ¼ **teaspoon dried thyme**
- 2 **tablespoons chopped fresh chives**
- 2 **tablespoons fresh lemon juice**
- 2 **teaspoons olive oil**
- 1½ **pounds sea scallops**
- ¼ **teaspoon black pepper**

Lemon zest (optional)

Heat a medium saucepan over medium-high heat. Coat pan with cooking spray. Add onion to pan; sauté 3 minutes.

Stir in pasta, broth, wine, and thyme; bring to a boil. Cover, reduce heat, and simmer 15 minutes or until liquid is absorbed and pasta is al dente. Stir in chopped chives and lemon juice. Keep warm.

While pasta cooks, heat a large cast-iron skillet over medium-high heat. Add oil to pan; swirl to coat. Sprinkle scallops evenly with pepper. Add scallops to pan; cook 3 minutes on each side or until desired degree of doneness. Serve with pasta mixture. Garnish with lemon zest, if desired. Serves 4 (serving size: 4½ ounces scallops and about ¾ cup pasta mixture)

Calories 373; Fat 4.5g (sat 0.9g, mono 2.1g, poly 0.5g); Protein 29.3g; Carb 50.9g; Fiber 2.3g; Chol 40mg; Iron 2.7mg; Sodium 542mg; Calc 29mg

Stir-fry this zesty shrimp dish for a quick weeknight dinner. Spoon over basmati or jasmine rice. Try the recipe with chicken or steak, too.

Shrimp *and* Broccoli Stir-Fry

HANDS-ON TIME: 11 min. **TOTAL TIME:** 11 min.

 PREP TIP *Slice the onion while the shrimp cooks, and you'll have this ready in less than 15 minutes.*

¼ cup fat-free, lower-sodium chicken broth

2 tablespoons rice vinegar

2 tablespoons lower-sodium soy sauce

2 teaspoons cornstarch

½ teaspoon dark sesame oil

¼ teaspoon crushed red pepper

1 tablespoon canola oil, divided

1 tablespoon bottled ground fresh ginger (such as Spice World)

1 tablespoon bottled minced garlic

1 pound peeled and deveined large shrimp

¼ teaspoon salt

4 cups small broccoli florets

1 cup vertically sliced onion

1 **Combine first 6 ingredients** in a small bowl, stirring with a whisk.

2 **Heat a large nonstick skillet** over medium-high heat. Add 2 teaspoons canola oil to pan; swirl to coat. Add ginger and garlic to pan; stir-fry 30 seconds. Sprinkle shrimp with salt. Add shrimp to pan, and stir-fry 3 minutes or until done. Remove shrimp mixture from pan.

3 **Add remaining 1 teaspoon canola oil to pan.** Add broccoli and onion to pan; stir-fry 4 minutes or until broccoli is crisp-tender. Add shrimp mixture and broth mixture to pan; cook 1 minute or until thickened, stirring constantly. Serves 4 (serving size: 1 cup)

Calories 220; Fat 6.7g (sat 0.8g, mono 2.4g, poly 1.9g); Protein 26.2g; Carb 11.8g; Fiber 2.8g; Chol 172mg; Iron 3.6mg; Sodium 577mg; Calc 105mg

 SIMPLE SWAP ◀ **For a vegetarian option, use tofu in place of the shrimp.**

Shrimp *and* Sausage Paella

HANDS-ON TIME: 11 min. **TOTAL TIME:** 18 min.

 PREP TIP *Saffron is expensive; fortunately, a pinch goes a long way. If you don't find chorizo sausage, use turkey kielbasa.*

- 2 **links Spanish chorizo sausage** (about 6½ ounces), cut into ½-inch-thick slices
- 1 **cup prechopped onion**
- 1 **cup prechopped green bell pepper**
- 2 **teaspoons bottled minced garlic**
- ¼ **teaspoon black pepper**
- ¼ **teaspoon crushed saffron threads**

- 1½ **cups instant rice**
- ¾ **cup water**
- ½ **teaspoon dried marjoram**
- 1 **(14.5-ounce) can no-salt-added diced tomatoes (undrained)**
- 1 **(8-ounce) bottle clam juice**
- 8 **ounces medium shrimp, peeled and deveined**

 **Heat a large nonstick skillet** over medium-high heat. Add sausage to pan; sauté 1 minute.

 **Add onion and bell pepper to pan;** sauté 4 minutes. Stir in garlic, black pepper, and saffron; sauté 1 minute.

 Stir in rice, ¾ cup water, marjoram, tomatoes, and clam juice; bring to a boil. Cover, reduce heat, and simmer 4 minutes or until rice is almost tender. Stir in shrimp. Cover and simmer 3 minutes or until shrimp are done. Serves 4 (serving size: about 1½ cups)

Calories 390; Fat 13.2g (sat 4.6g, mono 5.8g, poly 1.5g); Protein 23.3g; Carb 41.8g; Fiber 2.7g; Chol 114mg; Iron 5.1mg; Sodium 626mg; Calc 66mg

 SERVE WITH *A salad is all that's needed to complete the meal. Toss together 1 (5-oz) package arugula; 1 pint grape tomatoes, halved; 2 tablespoons fresh lemon juice, and 1 teaspoon olive oil. Serve immediately with the paella.*

Creole Shrimp *and* Rice

HANDS-ON TIME: 15 min. **TOTAL TIME:** 18 min.

PREP TIP *Using frozen chopped vegetables keeps the prep time to a minimum; however, you can use 1 cup chopped onion, 1/2 cup chopped green pepper, and 1/2 cup chopped celery, if needed.*

- 1 (3½-ounce) bag boil-in-bag long-grain rice
- 4 teaspoons canola oil, divided
- ¾ pound medium shrimp, peeled and deveined
- 1½ teaspoons Creole seasoning (such as Tony Chachere's)
- ⅛ teaspoon ground red pepper
- 2 cups frozen chopped green pepper, onion, and celery (such as Birds Eye)
- 1 tablespoon chopped fresh thyme
- 4 teaspoons bottled minced garlic
- 1 cup 1% low-fat milk
- 1 tablespoon all-purpose flour
- 2 cups cherry tomatoes, quartered
- ¼ teaspoon freshly ground black pepper
- 2 tablespoons minced fresh chives

1 **Cook rice** according to package directions, omitting salt and fat.

2 **While rice cooks,** heat a large skillet over medium heat. Add 2 teaspoons oil to pan; swirl to coat. Sprinkle shrimp evenly with Creole seasoning and red pepper. Add shrimp to pan; sauté 3 minutes or until browned, stirring occasionally. Remove from pan.

3 **Add 2 teaspoons oil to pan;** swirl to coat. Add chopped pepper mixture, thyme, and garlic; sauté 5 minutes. Combine milk and flour in a small bowl, stirring with a whisk. Add milk mixture to pan; bring to a simmer. Reduce heat to medium; cook 3 minutes or until slightly thickened. Add tomatoes and black pepper to pan; cook 2 minutes or until tomatoes are tender. Stir in shrimp; sprinkle with chives. Serve with rice. Serves 4 (serving size: 1¾ cups shrimp mixture and ½ cup rice)

Calories 283; Fat 7.3g (sat 1.2g, mono 3.6g, poly 1.9g); Protein 17.9g; Carb 36.7g; Fiber 4.1g; Chol 110mg; Iron 1.3mg; Sodium 699mg; Calc 164mg

SERVE WITH *Enjoy this spicy dish with a simple spinach salad: Gently toss fresh baby spinach leaves and thinly sliced red onion. Drizzle with a reduced-fat bottled balsamic vinaigrette.*

Jambalaya

HANDS-ON TIME: 9 min. **TOTAL TIME:** 24 min.

 PREP TIP *You'll find prechopped onion and celery in the produce department. If you don't have Cajun stewed tomatoes, add chopped green bell pepper, onion, and Cajun seasoning to stewed tomatoes.*

1½ cups quick-cooking rice, uncooked
1 teaspoon olive oil
1 cup prechopped onion
½ cup prechopped celery
1 tablespoon unsalted tomato paste
1 teaspoon dried basil
Dash of ground red pepper
1 tablespoon bottled minced garlic
1 bay leaf

2 (14.5-ounce) cans Cajun-recipe stewed tomatoes with pepper, garlic, and Cajun spices (such as Del Monte)
6 ounces andouille sausage, cut into ¼-inch-thick slices
1 (2-ounce) jar diced pimiento, drained
¾ pound peeled and deveined medium shrimp
2 teaspoons sliced green onions

1 **Cook rice** according to package directions, omitting salt and fat.

2 **While rice cooks,** heat a Dutch oven over medium-high heat. Add oil to pan; swirl to coat. Add onion and next 9 ingredients (through pimiento); cook 7 minutes or until vegetables are tender, stirring frequently.

3 **Stir in cooked rice and shrimp;** cook 6 minutes or until shrimp are done. Discard bay leaf. Sprinkle with green onions. Serves 6 (serving size: 1½ cups)

Calories 279; Fat 6.9g (sat 1.9g, mono 2.7g, poly 1.6g); Protein 20.5g; Carb 23.1g; Fiber 1.5g; Chol 84mg; Iron 2.9mg; Sodium 790mg; Calc 90mg

 SERVE WITH *This hearty New Orleans favorite is packed with vegetables, andouille sausage, and shrimp. Enjoy Jambalaya as a main dish at dinner, and then turn leftovers into lunch.*

Southern-Style Shrimp (pictured on page 68)

HANDS-ON TIME: 10 min. **TOTAL TIME:** 10 min.

 PREP TIP *Purchase peeled and deveined shrimp to save time. Then you'll only need to slice the green onions and chop the parsley while the shrimp cook.*

1 tablespoon butter

2 tablespoons bottled real bacon bits, divided

1 teaspoon bottled minced garlic

1 1/2 pounds peeled and deveined large shrimp

1 (8-ounce) package presliced mushrooms

1/2 cup sliced green onions

1/4 teaspoon salt

1/2 teaspoon hot pepper sauce

1/4 cup chopped fresh parsley

1 tablespoon fresh lemon juice

Fresh parsley (optional)

 Melt butter in a large nonstick skillet over medium-high heat. Add 1 tablespoon bacon bits and garlic; sauté 1 minute.

 Add shrimp; sauté 3 minutes. Add mushrooms; cook 1 minute or until mushrooms are tender and shrimp is done, stirring frequently.

Stir in onions, salt, and hot sauce; remove from heat. Stir in parsley and lemon juice. Sprinkle with 1 tablespoon bacon bits. Garnish with fresh parsley, if desired. Serves 4 (serving size: about 1 cup)

Calories 245; Fat 6.5g (sat 2.6g, mono 1.6g, poly 1.3g); Protein 38.6g; Carb 5.3g; Fiber 1.9g; Chol 269mg; Iron 4.9mg; Sodium 570mg; Calc 97mg

 SERVE WITH *For a taste of Southern goodness, serve this favorite over rice and with corn bread.*

Shrimp Scampi

HANDS-ON TIME: 10 min. **TOTAL TIME:** 10 min.

 PREP TIP *Peeled and deveined shrimp keep the prep time to a minimum.*

2 teaspoons olive oil

28 large shrimp, peeled and deveined (about 1½ pounds)

1 tablespoon bottled minced garlic

⅓ cup sauvignon blanc or other dry white wine

½ teaspoon salt

¼ teaspoon freshly ground black pepper

¼ cup chopped fresh flat-leaf parsley

1 tablespoon fresh lemon juice

 **Heat a large skillet** over medium-high heat. Add oil to pan; swirl to coat. Add shrimp; sauté 1 minute. Add garlic; sauté 1 minute.

 **Stir in wine, salt, and pepper;** bring mixture to a boil. Reduce heat to medium; cook 30 seconds.

3 **Add parsley and juice;** toss well to coat. Cook 1 minute or until shrimp are done. Serves 4 (serving size: 7 shrimp)

Calories 220; Fat 5.2g (sat 0.9g, mono 2.1g, poly 1.3g); Protein 34.9g; Carb 3.1g; Fiber 0.2g; Chol 259mg; Iron 4.5mg; Sodium 546mg; Calc 100mg

 SERVE WITH *Serve this Italian-style scampi over your favorite pasta with a side of Easy Corn Casserole (page 203) for a well-rounded meal.*

Greek-Style Scampi

HANDS-ON TIME: 10 min. **TOTAL TIME:** 10 min.

 PREP TIP *Due to its tiny circumference, angel hair pasta cooks in about 3 minutes. Look for cooked and peeled shrimp in the seafood section of your local market, or you can use frozen peeled and deveined shrimp.*

- **6 ounces uncooked angel hair pasta**
- **1 teaspoon olive oil**
- **1/2 cup prechopped green bell pepper**
- **2 teaspoons bottled minced garlic**
- **1 (14.5-ounce) can diced tomatoes with basil, garlic, and oregano, undrained**
- **1/8 teaspoon black pepper**
- **1 pound peeled and deveined medium shrimp**
- **1/8 teaspoon ground red pepper**
- **6 tablespoons (about 1 1/2 ounces) crumbled feta cheese**

1 **Cook pasta** according to package directions, omitting salt and fat. Drain, and keep warm.

2 **While pasta cooks,** heat a large nonstick skillet over medium-high heat. Add oil to pan; swirl to coat. Add green bell pepper to pan; sauté 1 minute. Add garlic and tomatoes; cook 1 minute.

3 **Add black pepper and shrimp;** cover and cook 3 minutes or until shrimp are done. Stir in red pepper; remove from heat. Place 1 cup pasta on each of 4 plates. Top each serving with 1 cup shrimp mixture and 1 1/2 tablespoons cheese. Serves 4

Calories 379; Fat 8.5g (sat 3g, mono 2.8g g, poly 1.7g); Protein 31.7g; Carb 43.3g; Fiber 2.6g; Chol 185mg; Iron 4.1mg; Sodium 139mg; Calc 656mg

 SIMPLE SWAP **Use chopped zucchini instead of green pepper.**

SERVE WITH

Make this a meal by serving it with ripe tomato wedges.

Gnocchi *with* Shrimp, Asparagus, *and* Pesto

HANDS-ON TIME: 15 min. **TOTAL TIME:** 15 min.

PREP TIP *This recipe is almost effortless when you purchase peeled and deveined shrimp. Gnocchi—small Italian potato dumplings—are a hearty alternative to pasta. You'll find vacuum-packed gnocchi in the pasta aisle. When cooking the gnocchi, start with hot water to decrease the time it takes the water to heat. While the gnocchi cooks, slice the asparagus. Begin step 3 as soon as you add the asparagus and shrimp to the pan—and dinner will be ready in 15 minutes flat.*

2 quarts plus 1 tablespoon water, divided

1 (16-ounce) package vacuum-packed gnocchi (such as Vigo)

4 cups (1-inch) sliced asparagus (about 1 pound)

1 pound peeled and deveined large shrimp, coarsely chopped

1 cup basil leaves

2 tablespoons pine nuts, toasted

2 tablespoons preshredded fresh Parmesan cheese

2 teaspoons fresh lemon juice

2 teaspoons bottled minced garlic

4 teaspoons extra-virgin olive oil

1 **Bring 2 quarts water to a boil** in a Dutch oven. Add gnocchi to pan; cook 4 minutes or until done (gnocchi will rise to surface). Remove with a slotted spoon; place in a large bowl.

2 **Add asparagus and shrimp to pan;** cook 5 minutes or until shrimp are done. Drain. Add shrimp mixture to gnocchi.

3 **While shrimp cook,** place 1 tablespoon water, basil, and next 4 ingredients (through garlic) in a food processor; process until smooth, scraping sides. Drizzle oil through food chute with food processor on; process until well blended. Add basil mixture to shrimp mixture; toss to coat. Serve immediately. Serves 4 (serving size: 2 cups)

Calories 355; Fat 9.3g (sat 1.6g, mono 4.5g, poly 2.5g); Protein 26.5g; Carb 42.7g; Fiber 3g; Chol 170mg; Iron 5.7mg; Sodium 747mg; Calc 108mg

+ SERVE WITH Plate over rice noodles or white rice. If you go with rice, short-grain rice cooks up moist, making it easier to eat with chopsticks.

Kung Pao Shrimp

HANDS-ON TIME: 10 min. **TOTAL TIME:** 20 min.

 PREP TIP *Like it hot? Simply add Sriracha (hot chile sauce, such as Huy Fong) to meet your taste.*

1 tablespoon lower-sodium soy
  sauce, divided

1½ teaspoons dry sherry, divided

2 teaspoons cornstarch

1 pound peeled and deveined
  medium shrimp

1 tablespoon peanut oil

¼ cup chopped dry-roasted
  peanuts

1 tablespoon bottled ground
  fresh ginger (such as Spice
  World)

1 tablespoon bottled minced
  garlic

½ teaspoon crushed red pepper

2½ cups frozen pepper, onion, and
  celery mix (such as Birds Eye)

¼ cup fat-free, lower-sodium
  chicken broth

1 teaspoon rice vinegar

¼ teaspoon salt

2 tablespoons sliced green
  onions

Chopped peanuts (optional)

1 **Combine 1 teaspoon soy sauce,** 1 teaspoon sherry, cornstarch, and shrimp.

2 **Heat a wok over high heat.** Add oil to pan; swirl to coat. Add peanuts and next 3 ingredients (through red pepper); stir-fry 30 seconds. Stir in bell pepper mix; stir-fry 2 minutes or until crisp-tender.

3 **Add shrimp mixture;** stir-fry 2 minutes. Add 2 teaspoons soy sauce, ½ teaspoon sherry, and broth. Bring to a simmer; cook 1 minute or until slightly thickened. Remove from heat; stir in vinegar and salt. Top with onions. Garnish with chopped peanuts, if desired. Serves 4 (serving size: 1¼ cups)

Calories 224; Fat 9.1g (sat 1.5g, mono 3.6g, poly 3.1g); Protein 25.9g; Carb 9.1g; Fiber 2.3g; Chol 172mg; Iron 3.4mg; Sodium 574mg; Calc 91mg

 SIMPLE SWAP If you'd like to add sliced mushrooms, simply decrease the pepper mixture. You'll have enough sauce for a total of 2½ cups vegetables. You can also use chicken or pork in place of the shrimp.

Shrimp, Peppers, *and* Cheese Grits

HANDS-ON TIME: 15 min. **TOTAL TIME:** 23 min.

 PREP TIP *There are three things that make this recipe quick and easy: peeled and deveined shrimp, prechopped frozen peppers, and quick-cooking grits. The result is only 15 minutes hands-on prep time.*

½ cup chopped Canadian bacon

2 cups frozen chopped bell pepper mix (such as Birds Eye)

1 (10-ounce) can diced tomatoes and green chiles, drained

1½ pounds medium shrimp, peeled and deveined

½ cup chopped green onions

1²/₃ cups fat-free milk

1 (16-ounce) can fat-free, lower-sodium chicken broth

1 cup uncooked quick-cooking grits

3 ounces shredded reduced-fat sharp cheddar cheese (about ¾ cup)

Jalapeño pepper slices (optional)

1 **Cook bacon in a skillet** over medium heat 3 minutes or until lightly browned, stirring frequently.

2 **Add bell peppers;** cook 10 minutes, stirring occasionally. Add tomatoes; cook 5 minutes. Add shrimp; cook 3 minutes. Stir in green onions; keep warm.

3 **While tomatoes cook,** combine milk and broth in a saucepan. Bring to a boil, and stir in grits. Bring to a boil; reduce heat, and cook 5 minutes or until thick, stirring occasionally. Stir in cheese. Serve shrimp mixture over grits. Garnish with jalapeños, if desired. Serves 4 (serving size: 1 cup grits and 1¼ cups shrimp mixture)

Calories 442; Fat 9.4g (sat 4.1g, mono 2.5g, poly 1.4g); Protein 46.5g; Carb 42.7g; Fiber 3.3g; Chol 223mg; Iron 5.7mg; Sodium 704mg; Calc 467mg

 SIMPLE SWAP **Use leftover chopped ham instead of Canadian bacon.**

Breaded Shrimp *with* Honey-Mustard Sauce

HANDS-ON TIME: 10 min. **TOTAL TIME:** 20 min.

PREP TIP

Prepare the breading and coat the shrimp while the pan heats. Heating the pan ahead helps create crispy "fried" shrimp without the fat from deep-frying.

Cooking spray

½ cup panko (Japanese breadcrumbs), toasted

¼ teaspoon garlic powder

⅛ teaspoon onion powder

Dash of salt

1 large egg white, lightly beaten

12 peeled and deveined large shrimp (about ¾ pound)

1 tablespoon whole-grain Dijon mustard

1 tablespoon honey

1 teaspoon orange juice

Dash of ground red pepper

Preheat oven to 400°. Coat a baking sheet with cooking spray; place pan in 400° oven for 10 minutes.

Combine panko, garlic powder, onion powder, and salt in a shallow dish, stirring with a whisk. Place egg white in another shallow dish. Dip shrimp in egg white, and dredge in panko mixture. Place on preheated baking sheet. Bake at 400° for 10 minutes or until done.

While shrimp bake, combine mustard and remaining ingredients. Serve sauce with shrimp. Serves 2 (serving size: 6 shrimp and about 1 tablespoon sauce)

Calories 140; Fat 1.0g (sat 0.2g, mono 0.0g, poly 0.2g); Protein 12.4g; Carb 21.0g; Fiber 0.6g; Chol 64mg; Iron 1.2mg; Sodium 298mg; Calc 16mg

SERVE WITH

Pair the shrimp with the homemade honey-mustard dipping sauce for an appetizer, or serve atop salad greens for a light supper.

Pizza Margherita,
page 104

4

pizzas, pastas & casseroles »

Say good-bye to boring grab-and-go fare with these options for quick-to-make favorites.

Pizza Margherita *(pictured on page 102)*

HANDS-ON TIME: 6 min. **TOTAL TIME:** 22 min.

 PREP TIP *Slice the tomatoes while the crust bakes so you'll be prepared to top the pizza when the crust is ready. Don't be tempted to skip the balsamic vinegar drizzle, as it blends together all the flavors.*

1 (10-ounce) can refrigerated pizza crust dough

Cooking spray

1 teaspoon extra-virgin olive oil, divided

1 garlic clove, halved

5 plum tomatoes, thinly sliced (about ³/₄ pound)

4 ounces sliced fresh mozzarella cheese (about 1 cup)

1 teaspoon balsamic vinegar

¹/₄ cup fresh basil leaves

¹/₈ teaspoon salt

¹/₈ teaspoon freshly ground black pepper

1 **Preheat oven to 400°.** Unroll crust dough onto a baking sheet coated with cooking spray; pat into a 13 x 11-inch rectangle. Bake at 400° for 8 minutes. Remove crust from oven, and brush with ¹/₂ teaspoon oil. Rub crust with cut sides of garlic.

2 **Arrange tomato slices on crust,** leaving a ¹/₂-inch border; arrange cheese slices over tomatoes. Bake at 400° for 12 minutes or until cheese melts and crust is golden.

3 **Combine ¹/₂ teaspoon oil and vinegar, stirring with a whisk.** Sprinkle pizza evenly with basil, salt, and pepper. Drizzle vinegar mixture evenly over pizza. Cut pizza into 8 slices. Serves 4 (serving size: 2 slices)

Calories 298; Fat 10g (sat 4.6g, mono 3.5g, poly 1.4g); Protein 12.2g; Carb 38.6g; Fiber 2.1g; Chol 22mg; Iron 2.6mg; Sodium 595mg; Calcium 175mg

 SERVE WITH *Serve with a fresh spinach salad topped with toasted pine nuts.*

Goat Cheese *and* Asparagus Pizza

HANDS-ON TIME: 3 min. **TOTAL TIME:** 15 min.

 PREP TIP *If you like a crispy crust, lightly coat the crust with cooking spray before adding the toppings.*

⅓ cup commercial pesto
1 (14-ounce) Italian cheese-flavored pizza crust (such as Boboli)
2 plum tomatoes, thinly sliced

8 asparagus spears, cut into 1-inch pieces
¾ cup (3 ounces) crumbled goat cheese

 Preheat oven to 450°.

Spread pesto over pizza crust, and top with tomatoes, asparagus, and cheese.

 Place pizza directly onto center rack in oven; bake at 450° for 10 to 12 minutes or until asparagus is crisp-tender and cheese melts. Cut pizza into 6 slices. Serves 6 (serving size: 1 slice)

Calories 301; Fat 14g (sat 6.9g, mono 1.1g, poly 5.3g); Protein 12.2g; Carb 31.2g; Fiber 1.7g; Chol 16mg; Iron 2.8mg; Sodium 543mg; Calc 257mg

Rustic Tomato-Olive Pizza

HANDS-ON TIME: 5 min. **TOTAL TIME:** 15 min.

 PREP TIP *Use parchment paper to keep your baking sheet clean and make cleanup easy.*

2 teaspoons yellow cornmeal

1 (14-ounce) Italian cheese-flavored pizza crust (such as Boboli)

Cooking spray

1 (28-ounce) can fire-roasted diced tomatoes, drained

4 ounces shredded mozzarella and Asiago with roasted garlic cheese blend (about 1 cup), (such as Sargento)

¼ cup sliced pitted kalamata olives

Chopped fresh oregano

1 **Preheat oven** to 450°.

2 **Cover a large baking sheet with parchment paper;** sprinkle with cornmeal. Place crust on top of cornmeal; lightly coat crust with cooking spray. Arrange tomatoes, cheese, and olives on crust.

3 **Bake at 450° for 10 minutes or until lightly browned** Sprinkle with oregano. Cut pizza into 8 slices. Serves 8 (serving size: 1 slice)

Calories 223; Fat 6.8g (sat 3.2g, mono 1.4g, poly 2.1g); Protein 9.5g; Carb 30.1g; Fiber 1.6g; Chol 8mg; Iron 1.9mg; Sodium 513mg; Calc 179mg

 SIMPLE SWAP Dress up this pizza with your favorite toppings, adding Canadian bacon, cooked chicken strips, or turkey sausage for a hearty option.

Enjoy this pizza with a simple side of fresh cucumber slices tossed with thinly sliced radishes, green onions, freshly ground black pepper, and your favorite vinaigrette.

Three-Cheese Veggie Pizza

HANDS-ON TIME: 4 min. **TOTAL TIME:** 18 min.

PREP TIP *Use this cheese pizza recipe as a template, and vary the cheeses and vegetables to make your own creations. Allow the pizza to stand five minutes before slicing; this gives any liquid on top time to reabsorb into the toppings so the crust won't get soggy. Sprinkle with crushed red pepper if you like it hot.*

2 teaspoons olive oil

¼ teaspoon freshly ground black pepper

2 teaspoons bottled minced garlic

1 (8-ounce) package presliced mushrooms

1 (14-ounce) Italian cheese-flavored pizza crust (such as Boboli)

Cooking spray

1 cup lower-sodium marinara sauce

2 ounces preshredded part-skim mozzarella cheese (about ½ cup)

1 ounce shredded fontina cheese (about ¼ cup)

1 ounce grated fresh Parmesan cheese (about ¼ cup)

¾ cup sliced bottled roasted red bell pepper

2 teaspoons capers, rinsed and drained

4 drained canned artichoke hearts, thinly sliced

1 **Preheat oven** to 500°.

2 **Heat a large nonstick skillet over medium-high heat.** Add olive oil to pan; swirl to coat. Add black pepper, garlic, and mushrooms; sauté 5 minutes or until mushrooms are tender and most of liquid evaporates.

3 **Place pizza crust** on a baking sheet coated with cooking spray. Spread sauce over pizza crust, leaving a ½-inch border; top with mushroom mixture. Sprinkle evenly with mozzarella, fontina, and Parmesan cheeses. Top with bell pepper, capers, and artichokes. Bake at 500° for 10 minutes or until cheese melts and begins to brown. Let stand 5 minutes before slicing. Cut pizza into 6 slices. Serves 6 (serving size: 1 slice)

Calories 345; Fat 11.5g (sat 5.4g, mono 4.1g, poly 1.1g); Protein 17g; Carb 42.2g; Fiber 1.6g; Chol 19mg; Iron 3.2mg; Sodium 576mg; Calcium 393mg

SIMPLE SWAP Fresh asparagus, grilled sliced vegetables, Canadian bacon, and meatless crumbles can be swapped for any of the toppings.

Spicy Sausage *and* Mushroom Pizza

HANDS-ON TIME: 12 min. **TOTAL TIME:** 27 min.

 PREP TIP *Using turkey rather than traditional pork sausage keeps the calories and fat down.*

1 (10-ounce) can refrigerated pizza crust dough

Cooking spray

4 ounces hot turkey Italian sausage

1 cup thinly sliced onion

1 (8-ounce) package presliced mushrooms

1 cup prechopped red or green bell pepper

½ cup lower-sodium marinara sauce (such as McCutcheon's)

2 ounces preshredded part-skim mozzarella cheese (about ½ cup)

1 ounce grated Parmigiano-Reggiano cheese (about ¼ cup)

1 **Preheat oven** to 450°. Unroll crust onto a baking sheet coated with cooking spray. Pat into a 12-inch circle.

2 **Heat a large nonstick skillet over medium-high heat;** coat pan with cooking spray. Remove casings from sausage. Add sausage to pan; cook 3 minutes, stirring to crumble. Add onion and mushrooms; sauté 4 minutes. Add bell pepper; sauté 2 minutes.

3 **Spread sauce over pizza crust, leaving a ½-inch border.** Top with sausage mixture. Sprinkle cheeses over sausage mixture. Bake at 450° on bottom oven rack for 15 minutes or until crust is golden. Cut into 6 slices. Serves 6 (serving size: 1 slice)

Calories 223; Fat 6.8g (sat 2.4g, mono 0.9g, poly 0.3g); Protein 12.5g; Carb 29.5g; Fiber 2.3g; Chol 19mg; Iron 3.7mg; Sodium 624mg; Calcium 145mg

Pizza Olympia

HANDS-ON TIME: 4 min. **TOTAL TIME:** 16 min.

 Bottled roasted red bell peppers taste delicious. They're often less expensive than fresh peppers, and they help to slash prep time. The feta cheese will not melt, so use the crust's golden color as an indicator of doneness.

1 (10-ounce) focaccia, cut in half horizontally

1 tablespoon bottled minced garlic

2 tablespoons tomato paste

2 teaspoons dried oregano

1 (7-ounce) bottle roasted red bell peppers, drained and chopped

½ cup prechopped red onion

1 tablespoon drained capers

4 ounces crumbled feta cheese (about 1 cup)

Preheat oven to 450°.

Place focaccia halves, cut sides up, on a baking sheet. Combine garlic, tomato paste, and oregano in a small bowl; spread evenly over focaccia halves. Top evenly with roasted pepper, onion, and capers; sprinkle with feta cheese.

Bake at 450° for 12 minutes or until focaccia is golden. Cut each pizza in half. Serves 4 (serving size: ½ pizza)

Calories 301; Fat 8.4g (sat 4.5g, mono 2.7g, poly 0.5g); Protein 11.4g; Carb 45.6g; Fiber 2.6g; Chol 25mg; Iron 3.2mg; Sodium 648mg; Calcium 160mg

SERVE WITH *Serve with a Greek salad: Combine a 10-ounce bag of mixed salad greens, ½ cup sliced cucumber, ½ cup sliced red onion, and 3 tablespoons crumbled feta cheese in a large bowl. Drizzle with low-fat Greek vinaigrette.*

The Works Pizza

HANDS-ON TIME: 6 min. **TOTAL TIME:** 18 min.

 PREP TIP *The meatless burger crumbles simply need to be heated, eliminating the step of browning meat for the pizza.*

1 (10-ounce) 100% whole wheat Italian cheese-flavored thin pizza crust (such as Boboli)

1 teaspoon olive oil

2 teaspoons bottled minced garlic

1 cup frozen meatless burger crumbles (such as Morningstar Farms)

1 cup prechopped onion

1 cup presliced mushrooms

⅓ cup prechopped green bell pepper

⅛ teaspoon salt

Olive oil–flavored cooking spray

⅓ cup tomato-basil pasta sauce (such as Classico)

6 ounces shredded part-skim mozzarella cheese (about 1½ cups)

1 **Preheat oven to 425°.** Place pizza crust directly on middle rack in oven while preheating.

 2 **While pizza crust bakes,** heat a large nonstick skillet over medium-high heat. Add oil to pan; swirl to coat. Add garlic and burger crumbles; sauté 2 minutes, stirring frequently, or until burger crumbles thaw. Add onion, mushrooms, and bell pepper; sauté 3 minutes. Remove from heat; sprinkle with salt.

 3 **Remove pizza crust from oven;** place on an ungreased baking sheet. Lightly coat crust with cooking spray. Spoon sauce over crust, leaving a 1-inch border around outside edge. Top with burger crumble mixture; sprinkle with cheese. Bake at 425° for 12 minutes or until cheese melts. Cut into 6 slices. Serves 6 (serving size: 1 slice)

Calories 260; Fat 9.3g (sat 5.2g, mono 3.5g, poly 0.4g); Protein 18.7g; Carb 30.2g; Fiber 5.3g; Chol 15mg; Iron 2.1g; Sodium 582mg; Calc 312mg

 SERVE WITH *Serve with a side salad of romaine lettuce and shaved Parmesan cheese.*

Pizza *with* Chicken *and* Artichokes

HANDS-ON TIME: 4 min. **TOTAL TIME:** 15 min.

PREP TIP *Pizza doesn't get much easier than this. Keep these ingredients in the pantry or freezer for easy pizza anytime.*

1 (10-ounce) Italian cheese-flavored thin pizza crust (such as Boboli)

1 (6-ounce) package diced cooked chicken breast

1¼ cups roasted garlic pasta sauce (such as Barilla)

1 (14-ounce) can quartered artichoke hearts, drained

1 cup prechopped green, yellow, and red bell pepper mix

2 tablespoons sliced ripe olives

3 ounces shredded part-skim mozzarella cheese (about ¾ cup)

1 **Preheat oven to 450°.** Place crust directly on oven rack (you do not have to wait for oven temperature to reach 450°); bake 9 minutes or until golden. Remove crust from oven, and place on baking sheet.

2 **Preheat broiler.** While broiler preheats, place chicken on a microwave-safe plate; microwave at HIGH 30 seconds.

3 **Spread pasta sauce over pizza crust.** Arrange chicken, artichoke hearts, bell pepper mix, and olives over sauce; sprinkle with cheese. Broil pizza 2 to 3 minutes or until cheese melts; serve immediately. Cut into 8 slices. Serves 8 (serving size: 1 slice)

Calories 221; Fat 6.3g (sat 4.2g, mono 0.8g, poly 1.1g); Protein 14.5g; Carb 26g; Fiber 2g; Chol 20mg; Iron 2mg; Sodium 503mg; Calc 137mg

Cuban Chicken Pizzas

HANDS-ON TIME: 10 min. **TOTAL TIME:** 12 min.

 Flour tortillas pinch-hit as a crisp crust for these hearty pizzas. Toasting the corn in a skillet brings out its natural sweetness and adds a deliciously smoky note. If you don't have cumin seeds, you can use ground cumin; just stir it constantly during the five seconds when toasting it in the skillet with the corn so that it doesn't burn.

4 (8-inch) fat-free flour tortillas

Cooking spray

1 (11-ounce) can no salt-added whole-kernel corn, drained

½ teaspoon cumin seeds

2 cups diced roasted chicken breast

1 (15-ounce) can black beans, rinsed and drained

1 teaspoon bottled minced garlic

2 tablespoons fresh lime juice

3 ounces shredded pepper-Jack cheese (about ¾ cup)

4 teaspoons chopped fresh cilantro

1 Preheat oven to 350°. Place flour tortillas on a baking sheet coated with cooking spray. Bake at 350° for 10 minutes or until edges are light brown. Remove from oven; stack and press down to flatten. Set aside.

2 While tortillas bake, heat a large nonstick skillet over medium-high heat; coat pan with cooking spray. Add corn to pan, and cook 1 minute or until lightly charred. Add cumin seeds; cook 5 seconds, stirring constantly. Add chicken, black beans, and garlic; cook 2 minutes or until thoroughly heated. Remove from heat; stir in lime juice.

3 Place tortillas on baking sheet. Spoon ¾ cup bean mixture onto each tortilla; top each with 3 tablespoons cheese. Bake at 350° for 2 minutes or until cheese melts. Sprinkle each pizza with 1 teaspoon cilantro. Serves 4 (serving size: 1 pizza)

Calories 460; Fat 10.2g (sat 4.8g, mono 2.9g, poly 1.7g); Protein 37.7g; Carb 54.3g; Fiber 8.4g; Chol 78mg; Iron 3.6mg; Sodium 660mg; Calcium 210mg

Mini White Pizzas
with Vegetables

HANDS-ON TIME: 6 min. **TOTAL TIME:** 15 min.

 PREP TIP *For a Greek-inspired variation, substitute hummus for the spreadable cheese.*

4 (6-inch) whole-wheat pitas
Olive oil–flavored cooking spray
1 medium zucchini, thinly sliced
¼ cup thinly sliced red onion, separated into rings
¼ teaspoon freshly ground black pepper

⅛ teaspoon salt
½ cup light garlic-and-herbs spreadable cheese (such as Alouette Light)
6 tablespoons shredded Asiago cheese

1 **Preheat broiler.** Place pitas on a baking sheet; broil 3 minutes.

2 **While pitas broil,** heat a nonstick skillet over medium-high heat; coat pan with cooking spray. Add zucchini, onion, black pepper, and salt; sauté 3 minutes or until vegetables are crisp-tender.

3 **Remove pitas from oven,** and spread 2 tablespoons garlic-and-herbs spreadable cheese over each pita. Top evenly with vegetables and Asiago cheese. Broil 3 minutes or until edges are lightly browned and cheese melts. Serves 4 (serving size: 1 pizza)

Calories 222; Fat 8.7g (sat 6.3g, mono 1.4g, poly 0.9g); Protein 11.9g; Carb 39.2g; Fiber 5.5g; Chol 24mg; Iron 2.2mg; Sodium 564mg; Calc 137mg

Maui French Bread Pizza

HANDS-ON TIME: 8 min. **TOTAL TIME:** 15 min.

PREP TIP *Use a serrated bread knife to smoothly cut the bread. This will make it easier to spread the sauce evenly over the loaf halves.*

1 (16-ounce) loaf French bread, cut in half horizontally
Cooking spray
1½ cups marinara sauce
¾ cup pineapple tidbits, drained
6 tablespoons deli ham, diced

1½ teaspoons bottled minced garlic
6 tablespoons sliced green onions
3 ounces shredded part-skim mozzarella cheese, divided (about ¾ cup)

1 **Preheat oven** to 450°.

2 **Cut each bread half crosswise into 3 pieces.** Coat cut sides of bread with cooking spray; place bread, cut sides up, on a baking sheet. Bake at 450° for 3 to 5 minutes or until lightly browned.

3 **Spread ¼ cup marinara sauce on each piece of bread.** Top each piece with 2 tablespoons pineapple, 1 tablespoon ham, ¼ teaspoon garlic, and 1 tablespoon green onions. Sprinkle each with 2 tablespoons cheese. Bake at 450° for 5 minutes or until cheese melts. Serves 6 (serving size: 1 piece)

Calories 291; Fat 4.6g (sat 2.3g, mono 1.2g, poly 0.8g); Protein 13.9g; Carb 49.4g; Fiber 2.2g; Chol 11mg; Iron 3.5mg; Sodium 645mg; Calc 166mg

Individual Canadian Bacon *and* Pineapple Pizzas

HANDS-ON TIME: 4 min. **TOTAL TIME:** 10 min.

PREP TIP

This recipe is great for any number of people because it's easily divisible or multipliable. If family members have favorite toppings, customize their individual pizza according to their tastes. Thoroughly drain the pineapple to avoid a soggy muffin.

6 **English muffins, split**

½ **cup tub cream cheese with pineapple**

6 **(³/₄-ounce) slices sandwich-style Canadian bacon, coarsely chopped**

¼ **cup sliced green onions**

1 **(8-ounce) can unsweetened pineapple tidbits, drained**

6 **ounces preshredded fat-free pizza-blend cheese (a blend of fat-free mozzarella and fat-free cheddar cheeses; about 1½ cups)**

1 Preheat broiler. Place muffin halves, cut sides up, on a large baking sheet. Broil 3 minutes or until lightly toasted.

2 Preheat oven to 425°.

3 Spread about 2 teaspoons cream cheese over each muffin half. Divide Canadian bacon, green onions, and pineapple tidbits evenly among muffin halves; sprinkle each with 2 tablespoons pizza cheese. Bake at 425° for 6 minutes or until pizza cheese melts. Serves 6 (serving size: 2 muffin halves)

Calories 373; Fat 8.9g (sat 4.7g, mono 2.7g, poly 1.1g); Protein 17.3g; Carb 39.9g; Fiber 0.2g; Chol 36mg; Iron 2.4mg; Sodium 701mg; Calcium 330mg

SERVE WITH

Add a side dish of corn for a super-fast, super-easy meal.

Linguine *with* Spicy Red Clam Sauce

HANDS-ON TIME: 10 min. **TOTAL TIME:** 10 min.

PREP TIP

Canned clams make this no-fuss linguine and sauce recipe super easy. Use less crushed red pepper or omit it, if you prefer a milder sauce. You can use dried herbs if you don't have fresh but remember the 3:1 ratio: 2 tablespoons fresh = 2 teaspoons dried, 1 tablespoon fresh = 1 teaspoon dried.

- 1 (9-ounce) package fresh linguine
- 1 tablespoon olive oil
- ½ cup prechopped onion
- 1 tablespoon bottled minced garlic
- ½ teaspoon crushed red pepper
- 2 tablespoons unsalted tomato paste
- 1 (14.5-ounce) can unsalted diced tomatoes, undrained
- 2 (6.5-ounce) cans minced clams, undrained
- 2 tablespoons chopped fresh parsley
- 1 tablespoon chopped fresh basil
- 1 tablespoon chopped fresh oregano

1 **Cook pasta** according to package directions, omitting salt and fat. Drain.

2 **While pasta cooks,** heat a large nonstick skillet over medium-high heat. Add oil to pan; swirl to coat. Add onion, garlic, and crushed red pepper to pan; sauté 3 minutes or until onion is lightly browned. Stir in tomato paste and tomatoes; cook 4 minutes or until thick, stirring constantly.

3 **Stir in clams;** cook 2 minutes or until thoroughly heated. Remove from heat; stir in parsley, basil, and oregano. Serve with pasta. Serves 4 (serving size: 1 cup pasta and about 1 cup sauce)

Calories 292; Fat 5.4g (sat 0.5g, mono 2.5g, poly 0.8g); Protein 15.5g; Carb 45.1g; Fiber 3.6g; Chol 17mg; Iron 3.9mg; Sodium 794mg; Calcium 47mg

SIMPLE SWAP You can use fresh littleneck clams, if you prefer. Cook them for about 5 minutes or until the shells open, and discard any unopened shells.

Tomato-Chicken Pasta

HANDS-ON TIME: 12 min. **TOTAL TIME:** 12 min.

 PREP TIP *If you don't have tomato sprinkles, use chopped sun-dried tomatoes packed in oil and eliminate the soaking step. Fresh basil makes all the difference in this dish. Cream gives the sauce a rich, silky finish.*

1 (9-ounce) package fresh fettuccine
¼ cup boiling water
2 tablespoons sun-dried tomato sprinkles
Cooking spray
2 teaspoons olive oil
½ cup finely chopped shallots
1 pound chicken breast tenders, cut into 1-inch pieces
½ cup dry white wine
⅓ cup whipping cream
½ cup chopped fresh basil, divided
1 ounce preshredded fresh Parmesan cheese (about ¼ cup)
½ teaspoon salt
¼ teaspoon freshly ground black pepper

1 **Cook pasta** according to package directions, omitting salt and fat.

2 **While pasta cooks,** combine ¼ cup boiling water and tomato sprinkles in a small bowl; let stand 5 minutes. Drain.

3 **While tomato soaks,** heat a large nonstick skillet over medium-high heat. Coat pan with cooking spray. Add oil to pan; swirl to coat. Add shallots and chicken; sauté 5 minutes. Reduce heat to medium; stir in wine and cream. Cook 3 minutes, stirring occasionally. Combine pasta, tomato, chicken mixture, ¼ cup basil, cheese, and salt, tossing well to coat. Sprinkle with ¼ cup basil and pepper. Serves 4 (serving size: 1½ cups)

Calories 374; Fat 13.3g (sat 5g, mono 6.2g, poly 0.9g); Protein 13.7g; Carb 51.1g; Fiber 3.8g; Chol 22mg; Iron 2.6mg; Sodium 632mg; Calc 212mg

 SERVE WITH *Enjoy with an arugula salad drizzled with your favorite dressing. Finish the meal with an easy strawberry parfait. Simply layer low-fat strawberry yogurt, sliced strawberries, and sliced banana in parfait glasses, and sprinkle with low-fat granola.*

Chicken *with* Pasta *and* Sun-Dried Tomatoes

HANDS-ON TIME: 10 min. **TOTAL TIME:** 10 min.

 For even faster prep, you can use frozen fully-cooked grilled chicken breast strips, found in your grocer's refrigerated and frozen food sections, omitting the ½ teaspoon salt.

8 ounces uncooked spaghetti
1 cup fat-free, lower-sodium chicken broth
1½ ounces sun-dried tomatoes, packed without oil (about 16)
1 pound skinless, boneless chicken breast, cut into thin strips
2 tablespoons dry white wine
1 teaspoon dried basil
1 teaspoon olive oil
¼ teaspoon salt
¼ teaspoon pepper
6 tablespoons shredded reduced-fat Monterey Jack cheese

1 **Cook pasta** according to package directions, omitting salt and fat.

2 **While pasta cooks, combine broth and tomatoes** in a 1-cup glass measure; cover with heavy-duty plastic wrap, and vent. Microwave at HIGH 3 minutes. Let stand, covered, 5 minutes. Drain tomatoes, and finely chop; set aside.

3 **While tomatoes cook,** place chicken and next 5 ingredients (through pepper) in a 2-quart casserole, and stir well. Cover with heavy-duty plastic wrap, and vent. Microwave at HIGH 4 to 5 minutes or until chicken is done, stirring after 2 minutes. Add tomatoes, pasta, and cheese; toss well. Serves 4 (serving size: 1¼ cups)

Calories 397; Fat 5.8g (sat 1.9g, mono 1.3g, poly 1g); Protein 37.6g; Carb 46.1g; Fiber 2.3g; Chol 73mg; Iron 3mg; Sodium 513 mg; Calcium 128mg

> **SIMPLE SWAP** ◀ Cook 12 ounces fresh spaghetti instead of 8 ounces dried pasta.

Fettuccine *with* Bacon, Peas, *and* Parmesan

HANDS-ON TIME: 10 min. **TOTAL TIME:** 10 min.

PREP TIP

Start cooking the pasta and bacon, and while those cook, chop the thyme and green onions to keep the start-to-finish time less than 10 minutes.

- 1 (9-ounce) package fresh fettuccine
- 2 smoked center-cut bacon slices
- 1/2 cup prechopped onion
- 2 teaspoons bottled minced garlic
- 1 tablespoon chopped fresh thyme
- 1/2 cup frozen green peas
- 1/2 cup chopped green onions
- 1/3 cup half-and-half
- 2 teaspoons butter
- 1/4 teaspoon salt
- 1/8 teaspoon black pepper
- 1 ounce shredded fresh Parmesan cheese (about 1/4 cup)

1 **Cook pasta** according to package directions, omitting salt and fat. Drain pasta, reserving 3/4 cup pasta cooking water.

2 **While pasta cooks, cook bacon** in a large nonstick skillet over medium heat until crisp. Remove bacon from pan, reserving drippings in pan; crumble. Add 1/2 cup chopped onion, garlic, and thyme to drippings in pan; sauté 2 minutes. Stir in peas; sauté 1 minute. Add green onions to pan, and sauté 1 1/2 minutes.

3 **Add pasta,** reserved pasta water, and half-and-half to pan; cook 1 minute or until thoroughly heated, tossing to combine. Remove from heat. Add butter, salt, and pepper to pan; toss until butter melts. Sprinkle with crumbled bacon and Parmesan cheese. Serves 4 (serving size: 1 1/2 cups)

Calories 313; Fat 9.9g (sat 4.5g, mono 3.8g, poly 0.4g); Protein 14.2g; Carb 43.1g; Fiber 3.7g; Chol 22mg; Iron 0.7mg; Sodium 600mg; Calc 145mg

SERVE WITH

Garlic bread and a romaine salad with grape tomatoes will complete the menu.

Tomato *and* Asparagus "Carbonara" *(pictured on cover)*

HANDS-ON TIME: 10 min. **TOTAL TIME:** 15 min.

 PREP TIP *Toss the pasta and vegetables immediately after cooking. The heat from the pasta will cook the egg, thickening it into a light, creamy sauce.*

- 8 ounces uncooked penne pasta
- 1 tablespoon extra-virgin olive oil
- 1 pound (1-inch) diagonally cut trimmed asparagus
- 1 tablespoon bottled minced garlic
- 1 pint cherry tomatoes, halved
- 2 ounces pecorino Romano cheese, finely grated (about ½ cup)
- ½ teaspoon kosher salt
- ½ teaspoon freshly ground black pepper
- 1 large egg
- ¼ cup fresh basil leaves

1 **Bring 3 quarts water to a boil in a Dutch oven.** Add pasta to boiling water; cook 10 minutes or until al dente.

2 **While pasta cooks,** heat a large nonstick skillet over medium-high heat. Add oil to pan; swirl to coat. Add asparagus; sauté 3½ minutes. Add garlic; sauté 1 minute. Add tomatoes; cook 6 minutes or until tomatoes are tender.

3 **Combine cheese, salt, pepper, and egg in a large bowl,** stirring with a whisk. Drain pasta, and immediately toss with egg mixture. Add tomato mixture, tossing until sauce thickens. Place pasta in each of 4 bowls. Sprinkle each serving with 1 tablespoon basil. Serve immediately. Serves 4 (serving size: 1¼ cups)

Calories 335; Fat 8.7g (sat 3.2g, mono 3g, poly 0.7g); Protein 14.7g; Carb 50.6g; Fiber 5.2g; Chol 63mg; Iron 4.8mg; Sodium 447mg; Calc 156mg

Garlicky Spaghetti *with* Beans *and* Greens

HANDS-ON TIME: 10 min. **TOTAL TIME:** 15 min.

Canned beans are a great pantry staple with lots of protein and fiber. To help reduce the sodium in regular canned beans, we rinse and drain them.

8 ounces uncooked spaghetti
³/₄ teaspoon kosher salt, divided
3 tablespoons extra-virgin olive oil
2 tablespoons bottled minced garlic
¹/₂ teaspoon crushed red pepper
2 cups grape tomatoes, halved

1 (16-ounce) can cannellini beans or other white beans, rinsed and drained
5 ounces arugula leaves
2 tablespoons fresh lemon juice
2 ounces grated fresh Parmesan cheese (about ¹/₂ cup)

1 **Cook pasta according to package directions,** omitting salt and fat. Drain pasta in a colander over a bowl, reserving ¹/₂ cup pasta cooking water. Place pasta in a small bowl. Add ¹/₄ teaspoon salt, tossing gently. Set aside, and keep warm.

2 **Return pan to medium heat.** Add oil, garlic, and pepper, and cook 2 minutes or until garlic is lightly browned, stirring occasionally. Stir in remaining ¹/₂ teaspoon salt, tomatoes, and beans; cook 2 minutes.

3 **Add pasta; cook 4 minutes, stirring frequently.** Add reserved pasta water and arugula, tossing gently to combine. Remove from heat. Stir in lemon juice and cheese. Serve immediately. Serves 6 (serving size: about 1¹/₂ cups)

Calories 290; Fat 10.5g (sat 2.7g, mono 5.8g, poly 1.3g); Protein 11.3g; Carb 38.1g; Fiber 3.7g; Chol 8mg; Iron 2.4mg; Sodium 469mg; Calc 173mg

SERVE WITH

Serve with Broccoli with Red Pepper Flakes and Toasted Garlic (page 195) and flax bread for a filling meal.

Spaghetti Carbonara

HANDS-ON TIME: 12 min. **TOTAL TIME:** 12 min.

 PREP TIP *This is a good use for leftover ham. Stir in thawed frozen green peas when you add the ham, if you'd like.*

12 ounces refrigerated spaghetti

1 cup chopped cooked ham

1½ ounces grated Parmigiano-Reggiano or fresh Parmesan cheese (about ⅓ cup)

¼ cup reduced-fat sour cream

¼ teaspoon salt

2 large eggs, lightly beaten

1 teaspoon bottled minced garlic

¼ teaspoon coarsely ground black pepper

 Cook pasta according to package directions, omitting salt and fat. Drain pasta in a colander over a bowl, reserving ½ cup pasta cooking water.

 Heat a large nonstick skillet over medium heat. Add ham, and cook 2 minutes or until thoroughly heated. Add pasta, and stir well.

 Combine cheese and next 4 ingredients (through garlic), stirring with a whisk. Add reserved pasta water to egg mixture, stirring with a whisk. Pour egg mixture over pasta mixture; stir well. Cook over low heat 5 minutes or until sauce thickens, stirring constantly (do not boil). Sprinkle with pepper. Serves 4 (serving size: 1 cup)

Calories 352; Fat 9.6g (sat 4.6g, mono 2.2g, poly 0.9g); Protein 21g; Carb 45g; Fiber 1.4g; Chol 139mg; Iron 1.7mg; Sodium 601mg; Calcium 179mg

Bow-Tie Pasta *with* Roasted Red Pepper–Cream Sauce

HANDS-ON TIME: 17 min. **TOTAL TIME:** 22 min.

Balsamic vinegar helps balance the natural sweetness of the red peppers. If you want a kick to the flavor, add crushed red pepper when sautéing the onions.

1 pound uncooked farfalle (bow-tie pasta)

2 teaspoons extra-virgin olive oil

1/2 cup prechopped onion

1 (12-ounce) bottle roasted red bell peppers, drained and coarsely chopped

2 teaspoons balsamic vinegar

1 cup half-and-half

1 tablespoon tomato paste

1/8 teaspoon ground red pepper

4 ounces shaved Parmigiano-Reggiano cheese, divided (about 1 cup)

Thinly sliced fresh basil (optional)

1 **Cook pasta** according to package directions, omitting salt and fat. Drain.

2 **While pasta cooks,** heat a large skillet over medium heat. Add oil to pan; swirl to coat. Add onion; stir and cook 8 minutes or until tender. Add bell pepper; cook 2 minutes. Increase heat to medium-high. Stir in vinegar; cook 1 minute or until liquid evaporates. Remove from heat; cool 5 minutes.

3 **Place pepper mixture in a blender;** process until smooth. Return pepper mixture to pan; warm over low heat. Combine half-and-half and tomato paste in a bowl; stir with a whisk. Stir tomato mixture into pepper mixture; stir with a whisk. Add ground red pepper. Combine pasta and pepper mixture. Add 1/2 cup cheese; toss. Spoon pasta mixture into each of 6 bowls.; top with cheese. Garnish with basil, if desired. Serves 6 (serving size: 1 1/3 cups pasta and about 1 1/2 tablespoons cheese)

Calories 424; Fat 10.7g (sat 5.6g, mono 3.7g, poly 0.5g); Protein 17.6g; Carb 62.9g; Fiber 3g; Chol 32mg; Iron 2.9mg; Sodium 383mg; Calcium 222mg

Pastitsio

HANDS-ON TIME: 15 min. **TOTAL TIME:** 19 min.

 PREP TIP *This easy beef-and-pasta dish features a creamy sauce that's sure to satisfy. Use any short pasta—ziti, rotini, and rigatoni also work. Add a dash of cinnamon, nutmeg, and allspice to the meat and cheese mixture for a change in flavor.*

8 ounces uncooked penne (tube-shaped pasta)
Cooking spray
1 pound ground sirloin
1 tablespoon olive oil
1½ cups prechopped onion
5 tablespoons bottled minced garlic
¼ teaspoon kosher salt
1 tablespoon all-purpose flour
2 cups fat-free milk
1 (14.5-ounce) can diced tomatoes, drained
½ cup (4 ounces) ⅓-less-fat cream cheese
1 (3-ounce) package fat-free cream cheese
3 ounces preshredded part-skim mozzarella cheese (about ¾ cup)
2 tablespoons chopped fresh flat-leaf parsley

 1 **Preheat broiler.** Cook pasta according to package directions, omitting salt and fat. Drain.

2 **While pasta cooks,** heat a large skillet over medium-high heat. Coat pan with cooking spray. Add beef to pan; sauté 5 minutes or until browned, stirring to crumble. Remove beef from pan; drain. Wipe pan clean with paper towels. Add oil to pan; swirl to coat. Add onion; sauté 4 minutes, stirring occasionally. Add garlic; sauté 1 minute, stirring constantly. Add beef; sprinkle with salt. Add flour; cook 1 minute, stirring frequently. Stir in milk, tomatoes, and cream cheeses, stirring until smooth; bring to a simmer. Cook 2 minutes or until thoroughly heated. Stir in pasta.

 3 **Spoon pasta mixture into a 13 x 9-inch** broiler-safe baking dish coated with cooking spray. Sprinkle mozzarella evenly over top. Broil 4 minutes or until golden. Sprinkle with parsley. Serves 6 (serving size: 1 ⅓ cups).

Calories 431; Fat 15.9g (sat 6.9g, mono 6.1g, poly 0.7g); Protein 27.8g; Carb 41.9g; Fiber 1.9g; Chol 61mg; Iron 2.4mg; Sodium 585mg; Calcium 289mg

 SERVE WITH *Enjoy this with a Greek salad and crusty Greek bread.*

 SIMPLE SWAP **Ground chicken, ground turkey, or soy crumbles can be used in place of ground sirloin.**

Lazy Lasagna

HANDS-ON TIME: 12 min. **TOTAL TIME:** 52 min.

 PREP TIP

Lasagna typically takes longer to put together than it does to cook. Precooked noodles and prepackaged convenience products, however, make this a zip to prepare. Be sure to cover the noodles entirely during baking to prevent them from drying out. You can substitute ground turkey or vegetarian crumbles for the beef.

1 pound ground round

1 (26-ounce) jar low-fat pasta sauce

1 (16-ounce) carton fat-free cottage cheese

2 tablespoons grated fresh Parmesan cheese

Cooking spray

1 (8-ounce) package precooked lasagna noodles

4 ounces preshredded reduced-fat mild cheddar cheese (about 1 cup)

Chopped fresh parsley (optional)

1 **Preheat oven** to 350°.

2 **Cook meat in a large nonstick skillet** over medium-high heat until browned, stirring to crumble. Drain well, and return meat to pan. Add sauce; bring to a boil. Reduce heat, and simmer 5 minutes. Combine cottage and Parmesan cheeses in a bowl; set aside.

3 **Spread ½ cup meat mixture in bottom of a 13 x 9-inch baking dish** coated with cooking spray. Arrange 4 noodles over meat mixture; top with half of cottage cheese mixture, 1 cup meat mixture, and ⅓ cup cheddar cheese. Repeat layers, ending with noodles. Spread remaining meat mixture over noodles. Cover and bake at 350° for 30 minutes. Uncover; sprinkle with ⅓ cup cheddar cheese, and bake 5 more minutes or until cheese melts. Let stand 10 minutes before serving. Garnish with parsley, if desired. Serves 9 (serving size: ⅑ of lasagna)

Calories 275; Fat 6.2g (sat 2.8g, mono 2.1g, poly 0.4g); Protein 28.1g; Carb 26.1g; Fiber 1.9g; Chol 43mg; Iron 2.8mg; Sodium 584mg; Calcium 181mg

 SERVE WITH

Serve with a light Caesar salad using a bag of torn romaine lettuce and low-fat Caesar dressing.

Beef *and* Cheese Macaroni

HANDS-ON TIME: 10 min. **TOTAL TIME:** 16 min.

 PREP TIP *Other short pastas work well, too, including penne, fusilli, and ziti. Use 8 ounces of any of them, and cook according to package directions, omitting salt and fat.*

8 ounces uncooked small elbow macaroni

1 pound ground sirloin

1¼ cups prechopped onion

2 teaspoons bottled minced garlic

1 (26-ounce) jar tomato-basil pasta sauce (such as Classico)

4 ounces reduced-fat shredded sharp cheddar cheese (about 1 cup), divided

1 **Cook pasta according to package directions,** omitting salt and fat. Drain and keep warm.

2 **While pasta cooks, heat a large nonstick skillet** over medium-high heat until hot. Add beef, onion, and garlic; sauté 6 minutes or until beef is browned, stirring to crumble. Drain, if necessary, and return beef mixture to pan.

3 **Add pasta sauce to beef mixture;** cook 2 minutes or until hot. Stir in pasta and ½ cup cheese; cook 1 minute or until cheese melts. Remove from heat; sprinkle with remaining ½ cup cheese. Serves 8 (serving size: 1 cup)

Calories 258; Fat 6.9g (sat 3.5g, mono 2.6g, poly 0.8g); Protein 20.4g; Carb 30.9g; Fiber 2.8g; Chol 38mg; Iron 2.5mg; Sodium 324mg; Calc 201mg

SERVE WITH

Serve with a mixed green salad tossed with cherry tomato halves and your favorite vinaigrette.

Easy Stovetop Mac and Cheese

HANDS-ON TIME: 15 min. **TOTAL TIME:** 20 min.

 PREP TIP *Penne or fusilli pasta can be used in place of the macaroni. Top with crumbled bacon for extra flavor, if desired.*

8 ounces uncooked large elbow macaroni

2 cups 1% low-fat milk

3 tablespoons all-purpose flour

$1/2$ teaspoon freshly ground black pepper

Dash of ground red pepper

3 ounces light processed cheese, shredded (such as Velveeta Light)

2.5 ounces preshredded extra-sharp cheddar cheese (about $2/3$ cup)

$1/4$ teaspoon kosher salt

Cooking spray

$1/4$ cup fresh breadcrumbs

1 **Preheat broiler.**

2 **Cook pasta** according to package directions, omitting salt and fat. Drain.

3 **While pasta cooks, combine milk, flour, and peppers** in a large saucepan, stirring with a whisk. Bring to a boil; cook 4 minutes or until thick. Remove from heat. Add cheeses and salt; stir until smooth. Add pasta, and stir to coat. Spoon mixture into a $1\frac{1}{4}$-quart broiler-safe glass or ceramic baking dish coated with cooking spray. Sprinkle breadcrumbs evenly over top; broil 2 minutes or until browned. Serves 4 (serving size: about $1\frac{1}{4}$ cups)

Calories 406; Fat 10.2g (sat 5.3g, mono 2.7g, poly 0.8g); Protein 20.6g; Carb 58.1g; Fiber 2.1g; Chol 33mg; Iron 2.3mg; Sodium 601mg; Calcium 300mg

Beefy Skillet Pasta

HANDS-ON TIME: 15 min. **TOTAL TIME:** 20 min.

PREP TIP *While the pasta cooks, brown the meat, which saves about 6 minutes total time.*

- **6 ounces uncooked fusilli (short twisted spaghetti)**
- **1 pound ground sirloin**
- **2 cups tomato-basil pasta sauce (such as Bertolli)**
- **¼ teaspoon freshly ground black pepper**
- **2 ounces shredded part-skim mozzarella or reduced-fat cheddar cheese (about ½ cup)**

1 **Cook pasta** according to package directions, omitting salt and fat. Drain.

2 **While pasta cooks,** cook beef in a large nonstick skillet over medium-high heat until browned, stirring to crumble. Drain and return beef to pan.

3 **Add pasta sauce and pepper;** cook 2 minutes. Add pasta; cook 2 minutes. Sprinkle with cheese; cook 1 minute or until cheese melts. Serves 5 (serving size: 1 cup)

Calories 305; Fat 9.8g (sat 5.5g, mono 3.1g, poly 1.1g); Protein 27g; Carb 28.2g; Fiber 2.9g; Chol 56mg; Iron 2.1mg; Sodium 543mg; Calc 175mg

SERVE WITH *Add a mixed greens salad to round out the meal.*

Tortellini *and* Broccoli Alfredo

HANDS-ON TIME: 5 min. **TOTAL TIME:** 15 min.

 PREP TIP *Start the sauce while the pasta cooks so that the sauce will be ready when the broccoli is done.*

1 (9-ounce) package refrigerated three-cheese tortellini

1 (12-ounce) package fresh broccoli florets

1 (1.6-ounce) envelope Alfredo sauce mix (such as Knorr)

1½ cups fat-free milk

2 teaspoons butter

⅛ teaspoon ground nutmeg

1 ounce preshredded fresh Parmesan cheese (about ¼ cup)

¼ teaspoon freshly ground black pepper

 1 **Cook pasta** according to package directions, omitting salt and fat; add broccoli during the last 3 minutes of cooking time. Drain well.

 2 **While pasta cooks,** prepare sauce mix according to package directions, using fat-free milk, butter, and nutmeg.

3 **Combine sauce and pasta and broccoli mixture;** toss well to coat. Top each serving evenly with Parmesan cheese and pepper. Serves 5 (serving size: 1 cup)

Calories 268; Fat 8g (sat 3.7g, mono 1.6g, poly 2.5g); Protein 15g; Carb 36.1g; Fiber 3.3g; Chol 27mg; Iron 1.5mg; Sodium 605mg; Calc 253mg

Turkey Tetrazzini

HANDS-ON TIME: 15 min. **TOTAL TIME:** 15 min.

 PREP TIP *If you use fresh pasta, start with 6 ounces instead of 4 ounces dried pasta.*

Cooking spray

1½ cups diced deli, lower-salt turkey breast (about ½ pound)

½ cup prechopped onion

1 cup fat-free, lower-sodium chicken broth

¼ cup water

4 ounces ⅓-less-fat cream cheese

2 ounces preshredded reduced-fat sharp cheddar cheese (about ½ cup)

4 cups hot cooked spaghetti (about 8 oz. uncooked)

2 tablespoons chopped fresh parsley

⅛ teaspoon black pepper

1 (2-ounce) jar diced pimiento

Parsley sprigs (optional)

1 **Heat a large nonstick skillet or saucepan** over medium-high heat. Coat pan with cooking spray. Add turkey and onion; sauté 3 minutes or until onion is tender.

2 **Stir in chicken broth, water, cream cheese, and shredded cheese;** reduce heat to low, and cook 3 minutes or until cheeses melt, stirring until mixture is smooth.

3 **Stir in pasta and next 3 ingredients;** cook until thoroughly heated. Garnish with parsley sprigs, if desired. Serves 4 (serving size: about 1¼ cups)

Calories 384; Fat 10.5g (sat 5.6g, mono 2.7g, poly 0.5g); Protein 25.4g; Carb 47.7g; Fiber 2.5g; Chol 49mg; Iron 2.3mg; Sodium 603mg; Calcium 180mg

 SIMPLE SWAP This is a great way to use a leftover cooked turkey or chicken. Canned tuna can also be used.

Chicken-Spaghetti Casserole

HANDS-ON TIME: 10 min. **TOTAL TIME:** 55 min.

 PREP TIP *Purchase rotisserie chicken to keep prep time to a minimum, or use cooked frozen diced chicken breast (such as Tyson). Break the pasta into small pieces to make it easier to toss. It will become tender during baking.*

- 2 cups chopped cooked chicken breast
- 3 cups uncooked spaghetti, broken into 2-inch pieces (about 7 ounces)
- 1 cup (¼-inch-thick) slices celery
- 1 cup prechopped red bell pepper
- 1 cup prechopped onion
- 1½ cups fat-free, lower-sodium chicken broth
- ½ teaspoon salt

- ¼ teaspoon freshly ground black pepper
- 2 (6.5-ounce) packages light Boursin cheese
- Cooking spray
- 4 ounces preshredded reduced-fat cheddar cheese, divided (about 1 cup)

1 **Preheat oven** to 350°. Combine first 5 ingredients in a large bowl.

2 **Combine broth, salt, pepper, and cheese** in a medium bowl, stirring with a whisk. Add cheese mixture to chicken mixture; toss. Spoon mixture into a 13 x 9-inch baking dish coated with cooking spray. Cover with aluminum foil coated with cooking spray.

3 **Bake at 350° for 35 minutes.** Uncover; stir and top with cheese. Bake 10 minutes more. Serves 8 (serving size: about 1 cup)

Calories 275; Fat 8.7g (sat 4.6g, mono 1.3g, poly 0.4g); Protein 24.7g; Carb 23.6g; Fiber 1.7g; Chol 46mg; Iron 1.3mg; Sodium 609mg; Calcium 182mg

SERVE WITH

Serve with sautéed spinach and ripe tomato wedges.

Gnocchi Gratin

HANDS-ON TIME: 6 min. **TOTAL TIME:** 26 min.

 Gnocchi are Italian dumplings, cooked and sauced like pasta. Here, they're turned into a creamy casserole that's quick and easy to prepare on busy days. Look for vacuum-packed gnocchi on the pasta aisle.

1 (22-ounce) package vacuum-packed gnocchi
1 tablespoon butter
1.5 ounces all-purpose flour (about ⅓ cup)
¼ teaspoon freshly ground black pepper
2 cups fat-free milk
½ cup fat-free, lower-sodium chicken broth
3 ounces shredded Gruyère cheese (about ¾ cup)
⅓ cup chopped fresh chives
2 bacon slices, cooked and crumbled
Cooking spray
1 ounce grated fresh Parmesan cheese (about ¼ cup)

1 **Preheat oven to 400°.** Cook gnocchi according to package directions, omitting salt and fat. Drain.

2 **While gnocchi cook,** melt butter in a large saucepan over medium heat. Add flour and pepper to pan; cook 1 minute, stirring constantly. Gradually add milk and broth, stirring with a whisk until blended. Bring to a boil; cook until thick, stirring constantly. Remove from heat. Add Gruyère, chives, and bacon; stir until smooth. Add gnocchi; toss well.

3 **Spoon mixture into an 11 x 7-inch baking dish** coated with cooking spray; sprinkle with Parmesan. Bake at 400° for 20 minutes or until lightly browned. Serve immediately. Serves 6 (serving size: about ¾ cup)

Calories 328; Fat 9.2g (sat 5.1g, mono 2.7g, poly 0.5g); Protein 14.1g; Carb 47.7g; Fiber 1.7g; Chol 29mg; Iron 1.3mg; Sodium 62 4mg; Calcium 304mg

 SIMPLE SWAP To make this dish vegetarian, use smoked gouda or smoked Gruyère cheese to replace the bacon flavor, and substitute vegetable broth.

Green Chile–Chicken Casserole

HANDS-ON TIME: 10 min. **TOTAL TIME:** 40 min.

 PREP TIP *You can use frozen diced chicken—just be aware that it contains more sodium, so you'll want to reduce the salt to ¹⁄₄ teaspoon.*

1¹⁄₃ cups fat-free, lower-sodium chicken broth

1 cup canned chopped green chiles, drained

1 cup prechopped onion

1 cup fat-free sour cream

¹⁄₂ teaspoon salt

¹⁄₂ teaspoon ground cumin

¹⁄₂ teaspoon freshly ground black pepper

2 (10.5-ounce) cans condensed 98% fat-free cream of chicken soup, undiluted (such as Campbell's)

1 teaspoon bottled minced garlic

Cooking spray

24 (6-inch) corn tortillas

4 cups shredded cooked chicken breast (about 1 pound)

8 ounces finely shredded sharp cheddar cheese (about 2 cups)

Chopped fresh flat-leaf parsley (optional)

1 **Preheat** oven to 350°.

2 **Combine first 9 ingredients** (through garlic) in a large saucepan, stirring with a whisk. Bring to a boil, stirring constantly. Remove from heat.

3 **Spread 1 cup soup mixture** in a 13 x 9-inch baking dish coated with cooking spray. Arrange 6 tortillas over soup mixture, and top with 1 cup chicken and ¹⁄₂ cup cheese. Repeat layers 3 times, ending with cheese. Spread remaining soup mixture over cheese. Bake at 350° for 30 minutes or until bubbly. Garnish with parsley, if desired. Serves 12 (serving size: about ³⁄₄ cup)

Calories 335; Fat 10.8g (sat 5.9g, mono 2.7g, poly 1.2g); Protein 23.9g; Carb 34.3g; Fiber 3.2g; Chol 66mg; Iron 1.5mg; Sodium 594mg; Calcium 270mg

Creamy Chicken *and* Broccoli Casserole

HANDS-ON TIME: 15 min. **TOTAL TIME:** 22 min.

 PREP TIP *Ready-to-use vegetables are the key to the ease of this casserole.*

- 1 (12-ounce) package steam-in-bag broccoli florets
- 1 tablespoon canola oil
- 1 cup prechopped onion
- 2 (8-ounce) packages presliced mushrooms
- 3 tablespoons all-purpose flour
- 1½ cups fat-free milk
- 12 ounces chopped skinless, boneless rotisserie chicken breast (about 3 cups)
- ½ cup plain fat-free Greek yogurt
- ¼ cup canola mayonnaise
- ½ teaspoon freshly ground black pepper
- ¼ teaspoon salt
- 2 ounces preshredded sharp cheddar cheese (about ½ cup)
- 1 ounce grated fresh Parmesan cheese (about ¼ cup)

1 **Preheat broiler.**

2 **Prepare broccoli** in microwave according to package directions.

3 **Heat a large ovenproof skillet** over medium-high heat. Add oil to pan; swirl to coat. Add onion and mushrooms; cook 12 minutes or until mushrooms brown and liquid evaporates, stirring occasionally. Sprinkle mushroom mixture with flour; cook 1 minute, stirring constantly. Stir in milk. Bring to a boil; cook 3 minutes or until thick and bubbly. Stir in broccoli and chicken; cook 1 minute. Remove pan from heat. Stir in yogurt, mayonnaise, pepper, and salt. Top evenly with cheeses; broil 2 minutes. Serves 6 (serving size: 1½ cups)

Calories 277; Fat 11.9g (sat 3.6g, mono 5.1g, poly 2.2g); Protein 29.1g; Carb 15.2g; Fiber 3.1g; Chol 66mg; Iron 1.5mg; Sodium 547mg; Calcium 253mg

Mushroom *and* Turkey Casserole

HANDS-ON TIME: 15 min. **TOTAL TIME:** 45 min.

 PREP TIP *This is ideal for leftover turkey and leftover gravy, but bottled gravy will work, too. Day-old bread is best for breadcrumbs, but you can bake fresh bread cubes in a 350° oven until toasted.*

1 (6-ounce) package long-grain and wild rice (such as Uncle Ben's)

1 ounce French bread or other firm white bread, cubed

1 tablespoon butter, melted and divided

3 ounces grated fresh Parmesan cheese (about ³/₄ cup)

¹/₂ cup prechopped onion

2 teaspoons bottled minced garlic

1 (8-ounce) package presliced mushrooms

1¹/₂ cups chopped cooked turkey

1 cup turkey gravy

¹/₂ cup 2% low-fat milk

¹/₂ cup reduced-fat sour cream

¹/₄ cup chopped fresh parsley

³/₄ teaspoon minced fresh or ¹/₄ teaspoon dried sage

¹/₄ teaspoon salt

¹/₄ teaspoon freshly ground black pepper

Cooking spray

³/₄ cup whole-berry cranberry sauce

 Preheat oven to 325°. Prepare rice according to package directions, omitting fat and seasoning packet. Set aside.

 While rice cooks, place bread in a food processor; pulse 15 times or until fine crumbs measure ¹/₂ cup. Add 1 teaspoon butter to processor; pulse until combined. Add cheese to processor, and pulse until combined.

Heat a large skillet over medium-high heat. Add 2 teaspoons butter, onion, garlic, and mushrooms; sauté 7 minutes or until onion is tender. Stir in turkey and next 7 ingredients (through pepper). Add rice; spoon into a 1¹/₂-quart casserole coated with cooking spray. Sprinkle with breadcrumb mixture. Bake at 325° for 30 minutes or until golden brown. Serve with cranberry sauce. Serves 6 (serving size: 1 cup casserole and 2 tablespoons sauce)

Calories 363; Fat 10.8g (sat 6g, mono 2.3g, poly 0.8g); Protein 23g; Carb 44.3g; Fiber 1.9g; Chol 62mg; Iron 2.6mg; Sodium 598mg; Calcium 268mg

SERVE WITH

Enjoy this with Warm Spinach Salad (page 213) for a family favorite meal.

Tuna-Noodle Casserole

HANDS-ON TIME: 7 min. **TOTAL TIME:** 22 min.

 PREP TIP *Put the water on to boil for the noodles first, as you'll want the noodles to be al dente by the time you're ready to add them to the tuna mixture.*

6 ounces uncooked egg noodles
1 tablespoon butter
³/₄ cup prechopped onion
1 cup fat-free milk
1 (8-ounce) tub reduced-fat cream cheese
1¹/₄ cups frozen green peas, thawed
1 tablespoon fresh lemon juice
¹/₄ teaspoon salt
¹/₄ teaspoon pepper
3 (4.5-ounce) cans low-sodium tuna in water, drained and flaked
1 (2-ounce) jar diced pimiento, drained
¹/₃ cup fresh breadcrumbs
2 tablespoons grated fresh Parmesan cheese

1 **Preheat oven to 450°.** Cook noodles according to package directions, omitting salt and fat. Drain.

2 **While noodles cook,** melt butter in a saucepan over medium-high heat. Add onion; sauté 3 minutes. Add milk and cream cheese. Cook 3 minutes; stir constantly with a whisk.

3 **Combine cream cheese mixture,** noodles, peas, and next 5 ingredients (through pimiento) in a 2-quart casserole. Combine breadcrumbs and cheese; sprinkle on top. Bake at 450° for 15 minutes or until bubbly. Serves 6 (serving size: 1 cup)

Calories 323; Fat 9.7g (sat 5.6g, mono 1.1g, poly 0.8g); Protein 26.3g; Carb 32.2g; Fiber 2.8g; Chol 66mg; Iron 2.7mg; Sodium 414mg; Calcium 219mg

Cheese-*and*-Bean Enchiladas

HANDS-ON TIME: 7 min. **TOTAL TIME:** 15 min.

 PREP TIP *You can top the bean mixture with shredded chicken or strips of cooked chicken before rolling up, if desired.*

1 (10-ounce) bag frozen chopped onion

1 (16-ounce) can fat-free refried beans with mild green chiles (such as Taco Bell)

8 ounces preshredded reduced-fat Mexican blend or cheddar cheese, divided (about 2 cups)

12 (6-inch) corn tortillas

1 (19-ounce) can enchilada sauce

2 tablespoons low-fat sour cream

2 tablespoons chopped ripe olives

6 tablespoons minced fresh cilantro

1 **Preheat oven** to 400°.

2 **Place onion in a sieve;** rinse with hot water. Drain well. Combine onion and beans in a microwave-safe bowl. Microwave at HIGH 3 minutes or until heated. Stir in 1 1/2 cups cheese.

3 **Stack tortillas;** wrap stack in damp paper towels, and microwave at HIGH 1 minute or until soft. Pour half of sauce in bottom of a 13 x 9-inch baking dish; dip both sides of each tortilla in sauce. Spoon about 1/4 cup bean mixture down center of each tortilla; roll up. Arrange tortillas in baking dish; top with remaining enchilada sauce and 1/2 cup cheese. Bake at 400° for 8 minutes or until thoroughly heated. Top each serving with sour cream, olives, and cilantro. Serves 6 (serving size: 2 enchiladas, 1 teaspoon sour cream, 1 teaspoon olives, and 1 tablespoon cilantro)

Calories 328; Fat 9.5g (sat 5.1g, mono 2.7g, poly 1.5g); Protein 18.4g; Carb 42.1g; Fiber 6.7g; Chol 15mg; Iron 2.7mg; Sodium 617mg; Calcium 400mg

Tamale Pie

HANDS-ON TIME: 5 min. **TOTAL TIME:** 18 min.

 PREP TIP *Homemade tamales are too time-consuming to prepare for weeknight meals; polenta approximates the flavor. Use a fork or pastry blender to crumble the firm polenta.*

1½ (16-ounce) tubes polenta, crumbled

Cooking spray

2 (15-ounce) cans low-fat turkey chili

4 ounces preshredded sharp cheddar cheese (about 1 cup)

6 tablespoons bottled salsa

6 tablespoons reduced-fat sour cream

1 **Preheat oven** to 475°.

2 **Place crumbled polenta** in an 11 x 7-inch baking dish coated with cooking spray. Top with chili and cheddar cheese.

3 **Bake at 475° for 13 minutes or until bubbly.** Top each serving with salsa and sour cream. Serves 6 (serving size: 1 piece tamale pie, 1 tablespoon salsa, and 1 tablespoon sour cream)

Calories 324; Fat 9.7g (sat 5.5g, mono 2.5g, poly 1g); Protein 18.8g; Carb 40.6g; Fiber 6.6g; Chol 46mg; Iron 2.8mg; Sodium 591mg; Calcium 223mg

 SERVE WITH *Start the meal with chips and salsa while the pie bakes.*

Ham *and* Potato Frittata

HANDS-ON TIME: 5 min. **TOTAL TIME:** 17 min.

PREP TIP

Use chicken in place of ham, if you prefer. If you have plain shredded frozen hash browns on hand, just add chopped onions and bell peppers to the mixture.

¼ cup 1% low-fat milk
¼ teaspoon salt
¼ teaspoon black pepper
4 large egg whites
3 large eggs

1 tablespoon canola oil
4 cups packaged frozen hash brown potatoes with onions and peppers (such as Ore-Ida Potatoes O'Brien)
1 cup chopped 33%-less-sodium ham

1 **Preheat oven** to 450°.

2 **Combine first 5 ingredients,** stirring with a whisk.

3 **Heat a large cast-iron or heavy ovenproof skillet** over medium-high heat. Add oil to pan; swirl to coat. Add potatoes; sauté 5 minutes. Stir in ham; sauté 1 minute. Stir in egg mixture. Bake at 450° for 12 minutes or until set. Cover and let stand 10 minutes. Cut into 8 wedges. Serves 4 (serving size: 2 wedges)

Calories 287; Fat 8.5g (sat 2.2g, mono 2.8g, poly 2.7g); Protein 17g; Carb 36.4g; Fiber 3.7g; Chol 172mg; Iron 3mg; Sodium 559mg; Calcium 67mg

SERVE WITH

Serve with fruit salad and toast for breakfast, or sautéed Swiss chard and garlic bread for later in the day.

Barbecued Chicken Hash

HANDS-ON TIME: 12 min. **TOTAL TIME:** 27 min.

 PREP TIP *Keep a bag of chopped peppers, onions, and celery in your freezer—you'll appreciate how convenient it is.*

1 1/2 tablespoons olive oil

2 cups frozen chopped peppers, onion, and celery (such as Birds Eye)

1/2 cup chopped carrot

4 cups chopped roasted skinless, boneless chicken breast (about 4 breasts)

3 1/2 cups frozen hash browns

3/4 cup water

1/2 cup barbecue sauce

1 teaspoon ground cumin

1 teaspoon chili powder

1/2 teaspoon bottled minced garlic

4 ounces preshredded reduced-fat sharp cheddar cheese (about 1 cup)

1 jalapeño pepper, seeded and minced

1 **Preheat oven** to 375°.

2 **Heat a large cast-iron or heavy ovenproof skillet** over high heat. Add oil to pan; swirl to coat. Add frozen chopped vegetables and carrot; sauté 1 1/2 minutes. Add chicken and next 6 ingredients (through garlic); bring to a boil. Reduce heat, and simmer 2 minutes.

3 **Bake at 375° for 10 minutes.** Sprinkle with cheese and jalapeño; bake an additional 5 minutes or until cheese melts. Serves 6 (serving size: 1 cup)

Calories 279; Fat 9.3g (sat 3.3g, mono 4.3g, poly 1g); Protein 25.1g; Carb 23.9g; Fiber 1.9g; Chol 59mg; Iron 1.4mg; Sodium 712mg; Calcium 212mg

 SERVE WITH *This hash is easy and comforting. A salad is all you need to turn it into a full meal.*

Tomato-Basil Soup, page 183
All-American Grilled Cheese
with a Twist, page 159

5

sandwiches & soups »

A hearty sandwich and a steamy bowl of soup are soothing favorites for a speedy meal.

Garlic-Thyme Burgers
with Grilled Tomato

HANDS-ON TIME: 10 min. **TOTAL TIME:** 18 min.

PREP TIP *Use a nonstick skillet if you don't have a grill pan.*

1 tablespoon chopped fresh thyme
³/₈ teaspoon kosher salt
¼ teaspoon freshly ground black pepper
2 teaspoons bottled minced garlic
1 pound ground sirloin

4 (½-inch-thick) slices beefsteak tomato
1 tablespoon fat-free mayonnaise
4 (2-ounce) Kaiser rolls or other sandwich rolls
4 baby romaine lettuce leaves

SERVE WITH *Enjoy this burger with an arugula salad drizzled with Italian dressing.*

1 **Combine first 5 ingredients** in a medium bowl. Divide mixture into 4 equal portions, shaping each into a ½-inch-thick patty.

2 **Heat a grill pan over medium-high heat.** Add patties to pan; cook 4 minutes on each side or until desired degree of doneness. Remove patties from pan.

3 **Add tomato slices to pan;** cook 1 minute on each side. Spread about ³/₄ teaspoon mayonnaise over bottom half of each roll; top each with 1 lettuce leaf, 1 patty, 1 tomato slice, and top half of roll. Serves 4 (serving size: 1 burger)

Calories 352; Fat 12g (sat 4.4g; mono 4.6g, poly 1.5g); Protein 28.5g; Carb 30.9g; Fiber 1.9g; Chol 73mg; Iron 4.7mg; Sodium 531mg; Calc 101mg

SIMPLE SWAP Basil leaves can be used instead of thyme.

Bacon *and* Cheddar Sliders

HANDS-ON TIME: 15 min. **TOTAL TIME:** 15 min.

 PREP TIP *Toasting the buns on the grill gives these little burgers a delightful crunch.*

3 tablespoons minced shallots

1 teaspoon Dijon mustard

12 ounces ground sirloin

3/4 teaspoon freshly ground black pepper, divided

Cooking spray

2 ounces shredded 2% reduced-fat sharp cheddar cheese (about 1/2 cup)

8 whole-wheat slider buns

3 tablespoons canola mayonnaise

4 cornichon or other small dill pickles, each cut lengthwise into 4 slices

4 small lettuce leaves, each torn in half

1 small ripe tomato, cut into 8 slices

3 cooked bacon slices, cut into 1-inch pieces

 Preheat grill to medium-high heat. Gently combine first 3 ingredients and 1/2 teaspoon pepper in a large bowl, being careful not to overmix. Divide beef mixture into 8 equal portions; gently shape each portion into a 1/4-inch-thick patty, taking care not to pack mixture down.

 Arrange patties on grill rack coated with cooking spray; cook 2 minutes on each side or until desired degree of doneness. Top each patty with about 1 tablespoon cheese during last minute of cooking.

Lightly coat cut sides of buns with cooking spray. Place buns, cut sides down, on grill rack. Grill 1 minute or until toasted. Spread about 1 teaspoon mayonnaise on bottom half of each bun; top with 1 patty. Top each slider with 2 pickle slices, 1/2 lettuce leaf, and 1 tomato slice; sprinkle evenly with remaining 1/4 teaspoon pepper. Arrange bacon pieces evenly over tomato. Top with bun tops. Serves 4 (serving size: 2 sliders)

Calories 400; Fat 16.9g (sat 4.9g; mono 6.4g, poly 4.2g); Protein 23.8g; Carb 39.8g; Fiber 5.9g; Chol 48mg; Iron 3.8mg; Sodium 783mg; Calc 290mg

 SERVE WITH *Serve with corn on the cob. Put the corn on the grill as you start the burgers.*

Mexican Chili-Cheese Burgers

HANDS-ON TIME: 14 min. **TOTAL TIME:** 25 min.

 PREP TIP *It's best to use plum tomatoes inside the burger, as they're less watery than other varieties. If you prefer to use fat-free cheese, you'll save about 4 grams of fat per burger. These can also be cooked in a grill pan over medium-high heat.*

1 pound ground round
1 cup chopped seeded plum tomato
¼ cup minced fresh cilantro
1 tablespoon chili powder
2 teaspoons minced seeded jalapeño pepper
½ teaspoon salt
½ teaspoon dried oregano
½ teaspoon ground cumin
¼ teaspoon black pepper
Cooking spray
4 (¾-ounce) slices reduced-fat Monterey Jack or cheddar cheese
¼ cup fat-free sour cream
4 (1½-ounce) hamburger buns
4 iceberg lettuce leaves
8 (¼-inch-thick) slices tomato
Grilled onions (optional)

1 **Combine first 9 ingredients** (through black pepper) in a bowl; stir well. Divide mixture into 4 equal portions, shaping each into a ½-inch-thick patty.

2 **Preheat grill to medium-high heat.** Place patties on grill rack coated with cooking spray; grill 6 minutes on each side or until done. Place 1 cheese slice on top of each patty; cover and grill an additional minute or until cheese melts.

3 **Spread 1 tablespoon sour cream over top half of each bun.** Place patties on bottom halves of buns; top each with 1 lettuce leaf, 2 tomato slices, onions (if desired), and top half of bun. Serves 4 (serving size: 1 burger)

Calories 381; Fat 13.1g (sat 5g; mono 6.4g, poly 0.7g); Protein 36.3g; Carb 28.1g; Fiber 1.7g; Chol 84mg; Iron 4.2mg; Sodium 655mg; Calc 212mg

 SERVE WITH *This will become your favorite "burger and fries" meal when served with oven fries.*

Chicken-Mozzarella Burgers

HANDS-ON TIME: 14 min. **TOTAL TIME:** 25 min.

PREP TIP *The marinara sauce makes the meat mixture somewhat soft, but it keeps the burgers moist when cooked.*

2 (3-ounce) square ciabatta rolls
1 garlic clove, halved
½ pound ground chicken
⅓ cup plus 2 tablespoons lower-sodium marinara sauce, divided
½ teaspoon chopped fresh rosemary
½ teaspoon chopped fresh thyme

¼ teaspoon crushed red pepper
⅛ teaspoon kosher salt
⅛ teaspoon black pepper
   Cooking spray
1 ounce shredded part-skim mozzarella cheese, divided (about ¼ cup)
8 basil leaves

1 Preheat broiler. Cut rolls in half. Place bread, cut side up, on a baking sheet. Broil 3 minutes or until lightly browned. Remove bread from pan. Rub each slice with cut side of garlic. Set aside.

2 Preheat oven to 375°. Combine chicken, ⅓ cup marinara, rosemary, thyme, red pepper, salt, and black pepper. Divide into 2 portions, shaping each into a ¼-inch-thick patty.

3 Heat an ovenproof skillet over medium-high heat. Coat pan with cooking spray. Add patties to pan; cook 3 minutes. Turn patties, and place pan in oven. Bake at 375° for 8 minutes. Top each patty with 2 tablespoons cheese; bake 1 minute. Layer bottom half of each roll with 2 basil leaves, 1 patty, 1 tablespoon marinara, 2 basil leaves, and roll top. Serves 2 (serving size: 1 burger)

SERVE WITH *Serve with baked sweet potato fries and a mixed berry compote.*

Calories 351; Fat 10.7g (sat 1.3g, mono 2.8g, poly 3.8g); Protein 14.8g; Carb 55.5g; Fiber 10.2g; Chol 83mg; Iron 7.3mg; Sodium 489mg; Calc 338mg

SIMPLE SWAP Swap out the herbs—try oregano. Shredded cheddar cheese is another option instead of mozzarella.

Double-Bean Burritos

HANDS-ON TIME: 8 min. **TOTAL TIME:** 8 min.

PREP TIP *To easily remove the pit from an avocado, use a 6- to 8-inch chef's knife. After the avocado is peeled and cut in half, insert the knife into the top where the stem was (it will be a darker area), and gently press down until you reach the pit. Gently scoop out the pit with a spoon. Prepare the avocado while the beans simmer.*

1 (3½-ounce) bag boil-in-bag brown rice
1 cup chunky bottled salsa
1 (15-ounce) can unsalted black beans, rinsed and drained
6 (10-inch) flour tortillas
6 tablespoons bean dip (such as Frito Lay)
3 ounces shredded Monterey Jack cheese with jalapeño peppers (about ¾ cup)
1 peeled avocado, cut into 6 slices
12 cilantro sprigs
6 lime wedges (optional)

1 **Cook rice** according to package directions, omitting salt and fat.

2 **While rice cooks, combine salsa and black beans** in a small saucepan; cook over medium heat 5 minutes or until thoroughly heated. Stack tortillas; wrap stack in damp paper towels. Microwave at HIGH 25 seconds or until warm.

3 **Spread 1 tablespoon bean dip over each tortilla;** top each tortilla with ¼ cup rice, ⅓ cup black bean mixture, 2 tablespoons cheese, 1 avocado slice, and 2 cilantro sprigs; roll up. Serve with lime wedges, if desired. Serves 6 (serving size: 1 burrito)

Calories 503; Fat 16.4g (sat 4.9g, mono 7.5g, poly 2g); Protein 16.1g; Carb 72.9g; Fiber 7.7g; Chol 18mg; Iron 4.1mg; Sodium 583mg; Calc 211mg

SERVE WITH *This is a one-dish meal that you can top with salsa. Enjoy it with unsweetened raspberry iced tea.*

Chicken *and* Bean Burritos

HANDS-ON TIME: 8 min. **TOTAL TIME:** 12 min.

 PREP TIP *For a flavor kick, add chopped jalapeños or a squirt of lime juice.*

- 2 teaspoons canola oil
- ½ cup prechopped onion
- 1½ teaspoons chili powder
- 1 teaspoon bottled minced garlic
- ½ teaspoon ground cumin
- ⅛ teaspoon salt
- ⅛ teaspoon freshly ground black pepper
- 12 ounces skinless, boneless rotisserie chicken, chopped
- ½ cup lower-sodium canned black beans, rinsed and drained
- 2 (10-inch) flour tortillas
- 1 ounce shredded Monterey Jack cheese (about ¼ cup)
- Cooking spray
- ½ cup pico de gallo
- ¼ cup reduced-fat sour cream

1 **Heat a large skillet** over medium-high heat. Add oil; swirl to coat. Add onion, chili powder, garlic, cumin, salt and pepper; sauté 3 minutes.

2 **Add chicken and beans;** cook 3 minutes or until heated through, stirring frequently. Divide chicken mixture evenly among tortillas. Top each burrito with 2 tablespoons cheese. Roll up each burrito jelly-roll fashion.

3 **Heat a large skillet over medium-high heat.** Coat both sides of burritos evenly with cooking spray. Place burritos in pan; cook 2 minutes on each side or until browned. Cut burritos in half. Top with pico de gallo and sour cream. Serves 4 (serving size: 1 burrito half, 2 tablespoons pico de gallo, and 1 tablespoon sour cream)

Calories 287; Fat 8.8g (sat 2.6g, mono 3.8g, poly 1.6g); Protein 24.7g; Carb 25.4g; Fiber 2.9g; Chol 57mg; Iron 2.4mg; Sodium 499mg; Calc 101mg

 SERVE WITH *Serve with baked tortillas chips and salsa. The chicken mixture is also tasty in tacos and quesadillas.*

Roasted Chicken–Artichoke Calzones

HANDS-ON TIME: 8 min. **TOTAL TIME:** 20 min.

 These calzones are a great way to use leftover chicken or deli rotisserie chicken. You can also purchase precooked chicken cut into strips (such as Perdue Short Cuts).

1 (14-ounce) can artichoke hearts, rinsed, drained and finely chopped

¼ teaspoon freshly ground black pepper

1 teaspoon bottled minced garlic

2 cups thinly sliced fresh spinach leaves

5 ounces shredded sharp provolone cheese (about 1¼ cups)

1 cup shredded cooked chicken breast (about 5 ounces)

1 teaspoon olive oil

2 teaspoons cornmeal

1 (13.8-ounce) can refrigerated pizza crust dough

1 **Preheat** oven to 425°.

2 **Pat artichokes dry with paper towels.** Combine artichokes, pepper, and garlic in a large bowl. Add spinach, cheese, and chicken; toss gently to combine.

3 **Brush oil over a baking sheet;** sprinkle with cornmeal. Unroll dough onto prepared baking sheet; cut into 6 equal portions. Pat each dough portion into a 6 x 5-inch rectangle. Spoon ⅔ cup spinach mixture into center of each dough portion. Fold one corner of each dough portion over spinach mixture to form a triangle. Press edges together with fingers to seal. Bake at 425° for 12 minutes or until golden. Serves 6 (serving size: 1 calzone)

Calories 347; Fat 11.6g (sat 4.6g; mono 0.9g, poly 0.3g); Protein 21.6g; Carb 40.1g; Fiber 4.8g; Chol 44mg; Iron 3.2mg; Sodium 698mg; Calc 222mg

 Let the calzones come to room temperature before wrapping to keep them from getting soggy. Pack some bottled marinara sauce for dipping. Use a microwave or toaster oven to reheat the calzones.

Tex-Mex Calzones

HANDS-ON TIME: 12 min. **TOTAL TIME:** 24 min.

Purchasing chopped onions and peppers gives you a jump start on preparing the calzones. Fire-roasted salsa verde is the secret to this recipe's great flavor; however, other salsas can be used instead.

 8 ounces ground turkey breast
½ cup prechopped onion
½ cup prechopped green bell pepper
½ cup prechopped red bell pepper
¾ teaspoon ground cumin
½ teaspoon chili powder
 2 teaspoons bottled minced garlic

½ cup fat-free fire-roasted salsa verde
 1 (11-ounce) can refrigerated thin-crust pizza dough
 3 ounces preshredded Mexican blend cheese (about ¾ cup)
Cooking spray
¼ cup fat-free sour cream

1 **Preheat** oven to 425°.

2 **Heat a large nonstick skillet over medium-high heat.** Add ground turkey, and cook 3 minutes, stirring to crumble. Add onion and next 5 ingredients (through garlic); cook 4 minutes or until vegetables are crisp-tender, stirring mixture occasionally. Remove from heat; stir in salsa.

3 **Unroll dough; divide into 4 equal portions.** Roll each portion into a 6 x 4-inch rectangle. Working with one rectangle at a time, spoon about ½ cup turkey mixture on one side of dough. Top with 3 tablespoons cheese; fold dough over turkey mixture, and press edges together with a fork to seal. Place on a baking sheet coated with cooking spray. Repeat procedure with remaining dough and turkey mixture. Bake at 425° for 12 minutes or until browned. Serve with sour cream. Serves 4 (serving size: 1 calzone and 1 tablespoon sour cream)

Calories 374; Fat 13.3g (sat 5g, mono 6.2g, poly 0.9g); Protein 13.7g; Carb 51.1g; Fiber 3.8g; Chol 22mg; Iron 2.6mg; Sodium 632mg; Calc 212mg

Steak *and* Cheese Sandwiches *with* Mushrooms

HANDS-ON TIME: 10 min. **TOTAL TIME:** 18 min.

 PREP TIP *You can use frozen chopped green pepper or frozen mixed pepper strips (green, yellow, and red) to trim a few minutes off the prep time. Toast the rolls, cut sides up, if you prefer them crusty.*

1 teaspoon olive oil
2 cups presliced onion
2 cups green bell pepper strips
2 teaspoons bottled minced garlic
1 cup presliced mushrooms
³/₄ pound top round steak, trimmed and cut into thin strips

¹/₄ teaspoon salt
¹/₈ teaspoon black pepper
2 teaspoons Worcestershire sauce
4 (0.6-ounce) slices reduced-fat provolone cheese, cut in half
4 (2¹/₂-ounce) hoagie rolls with sesame seeds

1 **Heat a large nonstick skillet** over medium-high heat. Add oil to pan; swirl to coat. Add onion, bell pepper, and garlic to pan; sauté 3 minutes. Add mushrooms to pan; sauté 4 minutes.

2 **Sprinkle beef with salt and black pepper.** Add beef to pan; sauté 3 minutes or until browned, stirring occasionally. Stir in Worcestershire sauce; cook 1 minute.

3 **Place 1 cheese slice half** on bottom half of each roll, and top each serving with one-fourth of beef mixture. Top with remaining cheese slice halves and tops of rolls. Serves 4 (serving size: 1 sandwich)

Calories 384; Fat 9.8g (sat 4.1g; mono 2.9g, poly 0.4g); Protein 32.9g; Carb 44.9g; Fiber 4.1g; Chol 43mg; Iron 4.7mg; Sodium 580mg; Calc 231mg

 TO GO *Cook the meat mixture and refrigerate until meal time, portioning out by individual servings. Reheat and assemble the sandwich just before eating.*

All-American Grilled Cheese *with* a Twist *(pictured on page 148)*

HANDS-ON TIME: 3 min. **TOTAL TIME:** 9 min.

 PREP TIP *Using a large skillet allows you to brown all the sandwiches at once.*

8 **(1-ounce) slices country white bread**

4 **ounces shredded sharp cheddar cheese (about 2 cups)**

8 **(¼-inch) slices plum tomato (about 2 tomatoes)**

¼ **cup thinly sliced fresh basil**

Cooking spray

 Place 4 bread slices on a work surface; arrange ½ cup cheddar cheese on each slice.

Top each slice with 2 tomato slices and 1 tablespoon basil. Top with remaining 4 bread slices.

 Heat a large nonstick skillet over medium heat. Coat pan with cooking spray. Add sandwiches to pan; cook 4 minutes or until lightly browned. Turn sandwiches over; cover and cook 2 minutes or until cheese melts. Serves 4 (serving size: 1 sandwich)

Calories 247; Fat 10.5g (sat 6.3g; mono 3.4g, poly 0.6g); Protein 11.6g; Carb 30g; Fiber 3.2g; Chol 30mg; Iron 1.1mg; Sodium 464mg; Calc 233mg

 SERVE WITH *Serve with a warm bowl of Tomato-Basil Soup (183) or as a stand-alone meal.*

Buffalo Chicken Panini

HANDS-ON TIME: 13 min. **TOTAL TIME:** 24 min.

PREP TIP

You don't need a panini maker for this easy, 5-ingredient sandwich—simply place a heavy skillet on the sandwiches and press down gently.

Cooking spray
¼ **cup hot pepper sauce, divided**
1 **pound chicken breast tenders**
½ **cup (2 ounces) crumbled blue cheese**

6 **tablespoons canola mayonnaise**
8 **(1-ounce) slices white or sourdough bread**

1 Preheat broiler. Coat broiler pan with cooking spray. Combine 2 tablespoons pepper sauce and chicken in a medium bowl, tossing to coat. Arrange chicken in a single layer on broiler pan; broil 4 minutes on each side or until done.

2 Place chicken in a bowl; toss with remaining 2 tablespoons pepper sauce. Combine cheese and mayonnaise. Spread 3 tablespoons cheese mixture on each of 4 bread slices; top each with one-fourth of cooked chicken and 1 bread slice.

3 Heat a grill pan over medium-high heat. Coat pan with cooking spray. Arrange 2 sandwiches in pan. Place a cast-iron or heavy skillet on top of sandwiches; press gently. Cook 3 minutes on each side or until bread is toasted (leave skillet on sandwiches while they cook). Repeat procedure with remaining 2 sandwiches. Serves 4 (serving size: 1 sandwich)

Calories 402; Fat 16.2g (sat 4.9g; mono 6g, poly 3.5g); Protein 32.4g; Carb 29.1g; Fiber 3g; Chol 75mg; Iron 0.8mg; Sodium 724mg; Calc 100mg

SERVE WITH

Serve with carrot sticks and hummus for dipping.

Grilled Cuban Sandwiches

HANDS-ON TIME: 4 min. **TOTAL TIME:** 8 min.

 PREP TIP *The trick to this easy sandwich is to cut the bread horizontally but not into servings until ready to cook. This lets you layer all the ingredients on the long loaf before cutting.*

4 teaspoons Dijon mustard
1 (8-ounce) loaf French bread, cut in half horizontally
4 ounces reduced-fat Swiss cheese, thinly sliced (such as Alpine Lace)
6 ounces deli, lower-salt ham
4 sandwich-sliced dill pickles
Cooking spray

 1 **Spread mustard evenly** over cut sides of bread.

 2 **Arrange half of cheese and half of ham** on bottom half of loaf; top with pickle slices. Repeat layer with remaining cheese and ham; cover with top half of loaf. Cut into quarters.

3 **Heat a large, heavy skillet over medium-high heat.** Coat pan with cooking spray. Add sandwiches; press with a heavy skillet (such as cast iron). Cook 2 minutes on each side. Serves 4 (serving size: 1 sandwich)

Calories 309; Fat 8g (sat 3.6g; mono 1.9g, poly 0.8g); Protein 19.1g; Carb 35.5g; Fiber 3g; Chol 33mg; Iron 2.8mg; Sodium 799mg; Calc 260mg

 TO GO *Cook the sandwiches, and then let them cool completely. Wrap them in foil, and reheat in a toaster oven.*

SERVE WITH

Round out the meal with a side of sweet potato chips, or enjoy it with rice and beans.

Pork Picadillo Sandwiches

HANDS-ON TIME: 10 min. **TOTAL TIME:** 15 min.

 PREP TIP *This version of the Cuban favorite uses pumpkin pie spice and chili powder to make short work of the usual long list of spices that go into traditional picadillo.*

1½ cups prechopped onion
1 teaspoon bottled minced garlic
1 pound lean ground pork
½ cup golden raisins
1 tablespoon chili powder
2 tablespoons red wine vinegar
1 teaspoon pumpkin pie spice
½ teaspoon salt
1 (28-ounce) can diced tomatoes, drained
¼ cup sliced pimiento-stuffed green olives
8 (1½-ounce) whole-wheat hamburger buns

1 **Cook onion, garlic, and pork** in a large nonstick skillet over medium-high heat 5 minutes or until browned, stirring to crumble. Drain and return mixture to pan.

2 **Stir in raisins and next 5 ingredients (through tomatoes).** Reduce heat, and cook 5 minutes, stirring occasionally. Stir in olives.

3 **Spread about ⅔ cup picadillo mixture** on bottom half of each bun; cover with top half of bun. Serves 8 (serving size: 1 sandwich)

Calories 289; Fat 9.2g (sat 2.5g; mono 4.2g, poly 1.9g); Protein 15.8g; Carb 37.7g; Fiber 3.3g; Chol 43mg; Iron 1.6mg; Sodium 754mg; Calc 64mg

 SIMPLE SWAP Ground chicken can be used in place of pork.

Ham *and* Spinach Focaccia **Sandwiches** *(pictured on page 7)*

HANDS-ON TIME: 8 min. **TOTAL TIME:** 8 min.

PREP TIP *Look for focaccia in the bakery section of your grocery store. If they don't have plain focaccia, feta cheese and spinach or tomato-basil focaccia are good flavor options.*

3 tablespoons canola mayonnaise

2 tablespoons chopped fresh basil

2 teaspoons sun-dried tomato sprinkles

¼ teaspoon crushed red pepper

1 (8-inch) round focaccia bread (about 8 ounces)

8 ounces deli, lower-salt ham, thinly sliced

1 (7-ounce) bottle roasted red bell peppers, rinsed, drained and sliced

1 cup spinach leaves

1 **Combine first 4 ingredients** in a small bowl.

2 **Cut bread in half horizontally.** Spread mayonnaise mixture over cut sides of bread.

3 **Place ham over bottom half of bread.** Top with peppers and spinach; cover with top half of bread. Cut sandwich crosswise into 4 wedges. Serves 4 (serving size: 1 wedge)

Calories 273; Fat 5.9g (sat 1.6g; mono 2.4g, poly 1.3g); Protein 17.3g; Carb 34.9g; Fiber 2.2g; Chol 29mg; Iron 2.6mg; Sodium 795mg; Calc 59mg

TO GO *This is a portable wrap-and-go meal. Cut the sandwich into wedges, and wrap each in plastic wrap. Keep refrigerated until ready to serve.*

Melty Monsieur

HANDS-ON TIME: 4 min. **TOTAL TIME:** 9 min.

 PREP TIP *Shave the cheese while the broiler preheats, and slice the tomato while the bread toasts—you'll have sandwiches in less than 10 minutes!*

4 (1½-ounce) slices multigrain bread

8 teaspoons creamy mustard blend (such as Dijonnaise)

8 Canadian bacon slices (4.8 ounces)

12 (¼-inch-thick) slices tomato

3 ounces shaved Gruyère cheese (about ¾ cup)

 1 **Preheat broiler.**

2 **Place bread in a single layer on a baking sheet;** broil 1½ minutes on each side or until lightly toasted. Spread 2 teaspoons mustard blend on each bread slice.

 3 **Top each serving** with 2 bacon slices, 3 tomato slices, and about 3 tablespoons cheese. Broil 3 minutes or until cheese melts. Serves 4 (serving size: 1 sandwich)

Calories 312; Fat 16.5g (sat 6.6g; mono 6.6g, poly 2.2g); Protein 19.7g; Carb 21.9g; Fiber 4.5g; Chol 48mg; Iron 1.4mg; Sodium 692mg; Calc 320mg

TO GO *Assemble the sandwiches without broiling them, and wrap them individually in plastic wrap. Just before eating, heat them under the broiler, in a toaster oven, or in the microwave until the cheese melts.*

Ham, Swiss, *and* Egg Sandwiches

HANDS-ON TIME: 6 min. **TOTAL TIME:** 9 min.

PREP TIP *It's quicker to split English muffins with a serrated knife, but if you prefer the "nooks and crannies" you can split them using a fork. Either way, split and toast them while the eggs cook.*

Cooking spray

4 ounces thinly sliced lower-sodium deli ham

4 large eggs

4 English muffins, split and toasted

4 (1-ounce) slices Swiss cheese

1
Preheat broiler.

2
Heat a nonstick skillet over medium-high heat. Coat pan with cooking spray. Add ham to pan; sauté 2 minutes or until lightly browned. Remove from pan. Recoat pan with cooking spray. Crack eggs into pan. Cover and cook 4 minutes or until desired degree of doneness. Remove from heat.

3
Place 4 muffin halves, cut sides up, on a baking sheet. Top each half with 1 cheese slice. Broil 2 minutes or until cheese melts. Divide ham among cheese-topped muffin halves; top each with 1 egg and 1 muffin half. Serves 4 (serving size: 1 sandwich)

Calories 344; Fat 14.7g (sat 6.7g; mono 4.1g, poly 1.5g); Protein 23.5g; Carb 29.1g; Fiber 0.0g; Chol 250mg; Iron 2mg; Sodium 553mg; Calc 351mg

SERVE WITH *Egg sandwiches are tasty any time of day. Pair these with orange juice for breakfast or a bowl of mixed fruit for lunch or dinner.*

Tex-Mex Chipotle Sloppy Joes

HANDS-ON TIME: 4 min. **TOTAL TIME:** 12 min.

If you like your Sloppy Joes less "sloppy," let the mixture simmer a few more minutes and continue to thicken. If you prefer a beefy "joe," use extra-lean ground beef instead of turkey.

1 teaspoon olive oil
½ cup prechopped onion
1 tablespoon bottled minced garlic
2 teaspoons canned minced seeded jalapeño pepper
1 teaspoon sugar
1 teaspoon ground cumin
1 teaspoon chili powder
½ teaspoon ground coriander
¼ teaspoon salt-free ground chipotle chile powder
1 pound ground turkey breast
1½ cups bottled mild salsa
1 tablespoon chopped fresh cilantro
4 (2½-ounce) Kaiser rolls, cut in half horizontally

1 Heat a large nonstick skillet over medium-high heat. Add oil to pan; swirl to coat. Add onion, garlic, and jalapeño; sauté 2 minutes or until soft.

2 Add sugar and next 5 ingredients (through turkey); cook 5 minutes or until turkey is browned, stirring to crumble. Stir in salsa; cook 4 minutes or until slightly thick. Stir in cilantro.

3 Spread about ¾ cup turkey mixture on bottom half of each roll; cover with top half of each roll. Serves 4 (serving size: 1 sandwich)

Calories 397; Fat 5.4g (sat 0.9g; mono 1.9g, poly 1.6g); Protein 35.4g; Carb 44.8g; Fiber 2.5g; Chol 70mg; Iron 4.1mg; Sodium 783mg; Calc 92mg

Make a quick black bean and corn salad to serve with the sandwiches. The turkey mixture can also be served over rice, or as a flavor-packed filling for tacos or enchiladas.

SERVE WITH *You may need a knife and fork to eat this sandwich. Serve with a side of cranberry sauce and sweet potato chips.*

Toasted Turkey *and* Brie Sandwiches

HANDS-ON TIME: 5 min. **TOTAL TIME:** 7 min.

 PREP TIP *Use a serrated knife to split the muffins to get a cleaner cut edge.*

4 **sourdough English muffins, split and toasted**

4 **teaspoons honey mustard**

2 **cups shredded cooked turkey breast (about ½ pound)**

¼ **cup thinly sliced red onion**

5 **ounces Brie cheese, sliced**

¼ **teaspoon salt**

¼ **teaspoon freshly ground black pepper**

½ **cup trimmed arugula**

 **1** Preheat broiler.

 2 **Arrange muffin halves, cut sides up, on a baking sheet.** Spread 1 teaspoon mustard over each of 4 halves; top each with ½ cup turkey and one-fourth of onion. Divide cheese evenly among remaining 4 halves.

3 **Broil 2 minutes or until cheese melts and turkey is warm.** Top turkey halves evenly with salt, pepper, and arugula. Top each turkey half with 1 cheese muffin half. Serves 4 (serving size: 1 sandwich)

Calories 340; Fat 11.6g (sat 6.8g; mono 3.1g, poly 0.7g); Protein 29.8g; Carb 28.8g; Fiber 2.3g; Chol 83mg; Iron 3.5mg; Sodium 686mg; Calc 174mg

 SIMPLE SWAP For a twist, try Cambozola cheese (a mixture of soft, rich Camembert and zingy Gorgonzola blue cheese) instead of Brie.

 **SERVE WITH** *Enjoy with carrot sticks and Tomato-Basil Soup (page 183).*

Grilled Turkey *and* Ham Sandwiches

HANDS-ON TIME: 9 min. **TOTAL TIME:** 9 min.

 PREP TIP *Vary this hearty grilled stacker with the meats you have on hand. For a flavor kick, use pepper-Jack cheese.*

1 tablespoon canola mayonnaise

1 teaspoon Dijon mustard

8 (1-ounce) slices country white bread

4 (1-ounce) slices deli, lower-salt turkey breast

4 (¹/₂-ounce) slices deli, lower-salt ham

4 (¹/₂-ounce) slices reduced-fat cheddar cheese

8 (¹/₄-inch-thick) slices tomato

Cooking spray

1 **Combine mayonnaise and mustard** in a small bowl.

2 **Spread about 1 teaspoon** mayonnaise mixture over 1 side of each of 4 bread slices. Top each slice with 1 turkey slice, 1 ham slice, 1 cheese slice, and 2 tomato slices. Top with remaining bread slices.

3 **Heat a large nonstick skillet** over medium heat. Coat pan with cooking spray. Add sandwiches to pan; cook 4 minutes or until lightly browned. Turn sandwiches over; cook 2 minutes or until cheese melts. Serves 4 (serving size: 1 sandwich)

Calories 237; Fat 5.8g (sat 1.8g; mono 0.9g, poly 0.9g); Protein 18.4g; Carb 29.1g; Fiber 0.4g; Chol 28mg; Iron 1.1mg; Sodium 781mg; Calc 166mg

SERVE WITH *Serve with a simple spinach salad and baked sweet potato fries. Start baking the fries first; by the time you heat the sandwiches, the fries will be ready.*

Open-Faced Turkey Sandwiches

HANDS-ON TIME: 7 min. **TOTAL TIME:** 7 min.

 PREP TIP *Serve these quick-to-make sandwiches whenever you have turkey and cranberry sauce left over and crave a hearty sandwich.*

4 (1-ounce) slices French bread

2 tablespoons canola mayonnaise

1 cup arugula

12 ounces sliced cooked turkey breast

4 reduced-sodium bacon slices, cooked and cut in half

½ cup whole berry cranberry sauce

2 teaspoons grated orange zest

2 tablespoons golden raisins

1 tablespoon chopped fresh parsley

1 **Preheat broiler.** Place bread slices on a baking sheet, and broil 2 minutes or until lightly toasted.

2 **Spread mayonnaise over bread slices.** Top with arugula, turkey, and bacon.

3 **Combine cranberry sauce, zest, raisins, and parsley.** Spoon over bacon. Serves 4 (serving size: 1 sandwich)

Calories 359; Fat 10g (sat 2.1g; mono 4.7g, poly 2.3g); Protein 32.1g; Carb 33.5g; Fiber 1.7g; Chol 82mg; Iron 2.7mg; Sodium 333mg; Calc 37mg

> **▷ SIMPLE SWAP ◁** Use deli-sliced turkey in place of a roasted turkey breast. Use cranberry chutney in place of the cranberry sauce-raisin mixture.

Ham *and* Mushroom
Quesadillas

HANDS-ON TIME: 4 min. **TOTAL TIME:** 13 min.

 PREP TIP *Flip the quesadillas gently during cooking so that the filling stays inside.*

Cooking spray
- 1 **cup chopped ham**
- 2 **tablespoons canned chopped green chiles**
- 1 **(8-ounce) package presliced mushrooms**
- 4 **(8-inch) flour tortillas**
- 4 **ounces shredded reduced-fat extra-sharp cheddar cheese (about 1 cup)**

 Heat a large nonstick skillet over medium-high heat. Coat pan with cooking spray. Add ham, green chiles, and mushrooms; sauté 5 minutes. Remove from pan. Wipe pan clean.

 Place 1 tortilla in pan. Sprinkle ¼ cup cheese over half of tortilla; arrange ½ cup ham mixture over cheese.

Cook 1 minute on each side or until cheese melts. Remove from pan; keep warm. Repeat procedure with remaining tortillas, cheese, and ham mixture. Serves 4 (serving size: 1 quesadilla)

Calories 245; Fat 6.5g (sat 2.3g; mono 2.6g, poly 0.8g); Protein 18.1g; Carb 28.7g; Fiber 0.8g; Chol 19mg; Iron 2.2mg; Sodium 802mg; Calc 221mg

 **SIMPLE SWAP** **Use chicken in place of ham and onion instead of the chiles for a fresh option.**

Four-Pepper Quesadillas

HANDS-ON TIME: 4 min. **TOTAL TIME:** 16 min.

PREP TIP *The pepper stir-fry with onion adds vibrant color. Using 1 cup chopped each of red and yellow pepper and ½ cup chopped onion is another option choice.*

1 (16-ounce) package frozen pepper stir-fry with onion, thawed
1 tablespoon finely chopped canned jalapeño pepper
½ teaspoon ground cumin
½ teaspoon salt
¼ teaspoon freshly ground black pepper
Cooking spray
8 (6-inch) corn tortillas
4 ounces shredded reduced-fat Monterey Jack cheese (about 1 cup)

1 **Combine pepper stir-fry mixture,** jalapeño pepper, cumin, salt and ground pepper, tossing gently.

2 **Heat a large nonstick skillet over medium-high heat.** Add stir-fry mixture. Cook 3 to 4 minutes or until heated, stirring frequently. Transfer to a bowl. Wipe pan clean.

3 **Heat skillet over medium-high heat.** Coat pan with cooking spray. Place 1 tortilla in pan, and top with ¼ cup bell pepper mixture. Sprinkle with ¼ cup cheese; top with 1 tortilla. Cook 2 minutes on each side or until golden, pressing down with a spatula. Repeat procedure with remaining tortillas, bell pepper mixture, and cheese. Serves 4 (serving size: 1 quesadilla)

Calories 225; Fat 7.2g (sat 3.4g; mono 1.9g, poly 0.9g); Protein 12.2g; Carb 30g; Fiber 4.3g; Chol 19mg; Iron 2mg; Sodium 558mg; Calc 327mg

▷ **SIMPLE SWAP** ◁ **Flour tortillas can be used instead of corn tortillas.**

Tangy Tuna-Salad Sandwiches

HANDS-ON TIME: 5 min. **TOTAL TIME:** 5 min.

 PREP TIP *Purchasing chopped vegetables allows you to just measure and combine, making it only five minutes from start to finish.*

½ cup prechopped red bell pepper

¼ cup bottled pickled vegetables, drained and chopped (such as Vigo Giardinera)

¼ cup prechopped red onion

¼ cup fat-free mayonnaise

1 (12-ounce) can low-sodium albacore tuna in water, drained and flaked

8 (1-ounce) slices multigrain bread

2 cups trimmed arugula or spinach

1 Combine first 5 ingredients in a medium bowl.

2 Spread ½ cup tuna salad over 4 bread slices.

3 Top each slice with ½ cup arugula and 1 bread slice. Serves 4 (serving size: 1 sandwich)

Calories 272; Fat 4.3g (sat 1g, mono 1.4g, poly 1.3g); Protein 21.3g; Carb 32g; Fiber 5.1g; Chol 33mg; Iron 2.9mg; Sodium 644mg; Calc 71mg

 SERVE WITH *This easy-to-make tuna recipe tastes great on bread as a sandwich or on top of lettuce as a salad.*

Peanut Chicken Noodle Soup

HANDS-ON TIME: 10 min. **TOTAL TIME:** 10 min.

 PREP TIP *If you can't find udon, substitute 6 ounces uncooked spaghetti. Slice the cabbage and chile while the chicken stock is heating.*

14 ounces uncooked fresh udon noodles

½ cup unsalted chicken stock

3 tablespoons reduced-fat creamy peanut butter

½ teaspoon kosher salt

½ teaspoon freshly ground black pepper

1 (13.5-ounce) can light coconut milk

3 cups shredded skinless, boneless rotisserie chicken breast (about 15 ounces)

3 cups thinly sliced napa cabbage

¼ cup cilantro leaves

1 small serrano chile, thinly sliced

2 tablespoons Sriracha (hot chile sauce, such as Huy Fong)

1 **Cook noodles according to package directions,** omitting salt and fat. Drain in a colander over a bowl, reserving 2 cups pasta cooking water.

2 **While noodles cook,** heat chicken stock and next 4 ingredients (through coconut milk) in a saucepan over medium-low heat.

3 **Add pasta water and chicken to milk mixture;** cook 3 minutes or until chicken is heated. Add noodles and cabbage; cook 2 minutes or until cabbage wilts. Sprinkle with cilantro and serrano; serve with Sriracha. Serves 6 (serving size: about 1¼ cups soup and 1 teaspoon Sriracha)

Calories 293; Fat 10.9g (sat 4.6g; mono 3.3g, poly 1.5g); Protein 25.1g; Carb 25.6g; Fiber 2.1g; Chol 73mg; Iron 1.7mg; Sodium 656mg; Calc 43mg

Chicken Noodle Soup

HANDS-ON TIME: 7 min. **TOTAL TIME:** 14 min.

PREP TIP

Heat the broth mixture in the microwave to jump-start the cooking. Meanwhile, sauté the aromatic ingredients in your soup pot to get this dish under way. You can use cut carrot "coins," which are available in many produce departments.

2 cups water
1 (32-ounce) carton fat-free, lower-sodium chicken broth
1 tablespoon olive oil
1/2 cup prechopped onion
1/2 cup prechopped celery
1/2 teaspoon salt

1/2 teaspoon freshly ground black pepper
1 medium carrot, chopped
6 ounces uncooked fusilli pasta
2 1/2 cups shredded skinless, boneless rotisserie chicken breast
2 tablespoons chopped fresh flat-leaf parsley

+ SERVE WITH *Make it a "soup and a sandwich" meal, pairing this with your favorite hoagie or submarine.*

1 **Combine 2 cups water and chicken broth** in a microwave-safe dish, and microwave at HIGH 5 minutes.

2 **While broth mixture heats,** heat a large saucepan over medium-high heat. Add oil to pan; swirl to coat. Add onion, celery, salt, pepper, and carrot; sauté 3 minutes or until almost tender, stirring frequently.

3 **Add hot broth mixture and pasta; bring to a boil.** Cook 7 minutes or until pasta is almost al dente. Stir in chicken; cook 1 minute or until thoroughly heated. Stir in parsley. Serves 6 (serving size: about 1 cup)

Calories 237; Fat 4.8g (sat 1g; mono 2.4g, poly 0.9g); Protein 22.9g; Carb 23.9g; Fiber 1.7g; Chol 50mg; Iron 1.8mg; Sodium 589mg; Calc 28mg

SIMPLE SWAP Though we like the shape of fusilli, you can also make this soup with wide egg noodles, rotini, or even orzo.

Egg Drop Soup

HANDS-ON TIME: 5 min. **TOTAL TIME:** 5 min.

 PREP TIP *Pour the beaten eggs through a sieve into the simmering broth to create the characteristic ribbons in the soup.*

4 cups fat-free, lower-sodium chicken broth

2 large eggs, lightly beaten

3 tablespoons chopped green onions

¼ teaspoon salt

 Place broth in a medium saucepan; bring to a boil. Reduce heat to low; place a wire mesh sieve over saucepan.

Strain eggs through sieve into pan. Remove from heat; stir in onions and salt. Serves 4 (serving size: 1 cup)

Calories 54; Fat 2.7g (sat 0.9g; mono 1.1g, poly 0.4g); Protein 5.7g; Carb 1.5g; Fiber 1.1g; Chol 106mg; Iron 1mg; Sodium 570mg; Calc 31mg

 SERVE WITH *Enjoy with Shrimp and Broccoli Stir-Fry (page 89).*

Black Bean Soup

HANDS-ON TIME: 4 min. **TOTAL TIME:** 4 min.

 PREP TIP *If you don't have a potato masher, mash the beans using the bottom of a drinking glass or measuring cup or the back of a large fork.*

2 (15-ounce) cans no-salt-added black beans, undrained

½ cup bottled salsa

1 tablespoon chili powder

1 (16-ounce) can fat-free, lower-sodium chicken broth

2 ounces shredded reduced-fat sharp cheddar cheese (about ½ cup)

5 tablespoons low-fat sour cream

5 tablespoons minced green onions

2½ tablespoons chopped fresh cilantro

1 **Place beans and liquid in a medium saucepan;** partially mash beans with a potato masher.

2 **Place over high heat;** stir in salsa, chili powder, and broth. Bring to a boil.

3 **Ladle soup into each of 5 bowls;** top with cheese, sour cream, onions, and cilantro. Serves 5 (serving size: 1 cup soup, 1½ tablespoons cheese, 1 tablespoon sour cream, 1 tablespoon onions, and 1½ teaspoons cilantro)

Calories 212; Fat 4.9g (sat 2.6g, mono 1.2g, poly 0.5g); Protein 14.7g; Carb 28.7g; Fiber 5.4g; Chol 13mg; Iron 2.9mg; Sodium 411mg; Calc 163mg

 SERVE WITH *Enjoy this quick soup with Four-Pepper Quesadillas (page 175) or with toasted tortilla wedges.*

Thai Butternut Soup

HANDS-ON TIME: 13 min. **TOTAL TIME:** 18 min.

PREP TIP *If you can't find frozen pureed squash, you can cook this soup with 4 cups cubed butternut squash. Just add five extra minutes to the cooking time in step 2. While the lime juice may surprise you, don't leave it out, as it brings all the flavors together.*

1 teaspoon canola oil
1 cup chopped onion
2½ teaspoons red curry paste
1½ teaspoons bottled minced garlic
1 teaspoon minced fresh ginger
1 cup fat-free, lower-sodium chicken broth
2 teaspoons brown sugar
2 (12-ounce) packages frozen pureed butternut squash

1 (14-ounce) can light coconut milk
1½ teaspoons fish sauce
¼ teaspoon salt
½ cup chopped unsalted, dry-roasted peanuts
¼ cup cilantro leaves
1 lime, cut into 8 wedges

1 **Heat a medium saucepan** over medium-high heat. Add oil; swirl to coat. Add onion; sauté 3 minutes. Add curry paste, garlic, and ginger; sauté 45 seconds, stirring constantly.

2 **Add broth and next 5 ingredients (through salt); cover.** Bring to a boil. Reduce heat, and simmer 5 minutes, stirring frequently.

3 **Place half of squash mixture in a blender.** Remove center piece of blender lid (to allow steam to escape); secure blender lid on blender. Place a clean towel over opening in blender lid (to avoid splatters). Blend until smooth. Pour into a large bowl. Repeat procedure with remaining squash mixture. Ladle soup into each of 4 bowls; top with peanuts and cilantro. Serve with lime wedges. Serves 4 (serving size: about 1 cup soup, 2 tablespoons peanuts, 1 tablespoon cilantro, and 2 lime wedges)

+ SERVE WITH *Serve with Curry-Chutney Snapper (page 78) and basmati rice.*

Calories 302; Fat 15.2g (sat 5.7g; mono 5.3g, poly 3.3g); Protein 9.5g; Carb 40.7g; Fiber 4.9g; Chol 0.0mg; Iron 2.7mg; Sodium 591mg; Calc 81mg

Tomato-Basil Soup
with Cheese Toast

HANDS-ON TIME: 15 min. **TOTAL TIME:** 15 min.

PREP TIP *If you have an immersion blender, use it to chop the tomatoes—it's quick and saves cleanup time.*

1 tablespoon extra-virgin olive oil

1½ cups prechopped onion

1 tablespoon bottled minced garlic

¾ cup chopped fresh basil

1 (28-ounce) can fire-roasted diced tomatoes, undrained

½ cup (4 ounces) ⅓-less-fat cream cheese, cut into cubes

2 cups 1% low-fat milk

¼ teaspoon salt

¼ teaspoon black pepper

12 (½-inch-thick) slices French bread

Cooking spray

1 garlic clove, halved

1 ounce shredded Asiago cheese (about ¼ cup)

Preheat broiler.

Heat a saucepan over medium-high heat. Add olive oil to pan; swirl to coat. Add onion; sauté 3 minutes. Stir in garlic; cook 1 minute. Add basil and tomatoes; bring to a boil. Remove from heat. Stir in cream cheese until melted. Place mixture in blender; blend until smooth. Return to pan; stir in milk, salt, and pepper. Cook over medium heat 2 minutes.

While soup cooks, place bread on a baking sheet; lightly coat with cooking spray. Broil 1 minute. Rub garlic over toasted side; turn bread over. Top with Asiago; broil 1 minute. Serves 4 (serving size: 1¼ cups soup and 3 toasts)

Calories 312; Fat 13.9g (sat 6.3g; mono 4.5g, poly 0.9g); Protein 13.2g; Carb 33.8g; Fiber 3.4g; Chol 33mg; Iron 1.4mg; Sodium 506mg; Calc 281mg

SERVE WITH *Tomato-Basil Soup gets a jump start with a can of fire-roasted tomatoes. Pair it with a salad, or omit the cheese toast and add your favorite grilled cheese sandwich.*

Loaded Smashed Potato Soup

HANDS-ON TIME: 14 min. **TOTAL TIME:** 20 min.

 PREP TIP *No need to peel the potatoes. Leaving the skins on saves time and adds texure to the soup.*

4 (6-ounce) red potatoes
2 teaspoons olive oil
½ cup prechopped onion
1¼ cups fat-free, lower-sodium chicken broth
3 tablespoons all-purpose flour
2 cups 1% low-fat milk, divided
¼ cup reduced-fat sour cream
¼ teaspoon salt
¼ teaspoon freshly ground black pepper
3 bacon slices, halved
1½ ounces shredded cheddar cheese (about ⅓ cup)
4 teaspoons thinly sliced green onions

1 **Pierce potatoes with a fork.** Microwave at HIGH 13 minutes or until tender. Cut in half; cool slightly.

2 **While potatoes cook,** heat a saucepan over medium-high heat. Add oil to pan; swirl to coat. Add onion; sauté 3 minutes. Add broth. Combine flour and ½ cup milk; add to pan with 1½ cups milk. Bring to a boil; stir often. Cook 1 minute. Remove from heat; stir in sour cream, salt, and pepper.

3 **Arrange bacon on a paper towel on a microwave-safe plate.** Cover with a paper towel; microwave at HIGH 4 minutes. Crumble bacon. Add potatoes to broth mixture. Coarsely mash potatoes into soup. Top with cheese, green onions, and bacon. Serves 4 (serving size: about 1¼ cups)

Calories 325; Fat 11.1g (sat 5.2g; mono 4.5g, poly 0.8g); Protein 13.2g; Carb 43.8g; Fiber 3g; Chol 27mg; Iron 1.3mg; Sodium 523mg; Calc 261mg

 SERVE WITH *Kids of all ages will enjoy topping this soup with bacon and cheese. You'll have time to make a salad while the potatoes cook. Serve your favorite greens tossed with a zesty dressing.*

Broccoli *and* Cheese Soup

HANDS-ON TIME: 5 min. **TOTAL TIME:** 24 min.

 PREP TIP *Processed cheese melts beautifully, giving this soup a smooth texture and mild flavor.*

Cooking spray
1 cup prechopped onion
2 teaspoons bottled minced garlic
3 cups fat-free, lower-sodium chicken broth
1 (16-ounce) package broccoli florets

2½ cups 2% reduced-fat milk
1.5 ounces all-purpose flour (about ⅓ cup)
¼ teaspoon black pepper
7 ounces light processed cheese, cubed (such as Velveeta Light)

1 **Heat a large nonstick saucepan** over medium-high heat. Coat pan with cooking spray. Add onion and garlic; sauté 3 minutes or until tender. Add broth and broccoli. Bring broccoli mixture to a boil over medium-high heat. Reduce heat to medium; cook 10 minutes.

2 **Combine milk and flour,** stirring with a whisk until well blended. Add milk mixture to broccoli mixture. Cook 5 minutes or until slightly thick, stirring constantly. Stir in pepper. Remove from heat; add cheese, stirring until cheese melts.

3 **Place one-third of soup** in a blender or food processor, and process until smooth. Return pureed soup mixture to pan. Serves 6 (serving size: 1⅓ cups)

Calories 195; Fat 6.2g (sat 3g, mono 1.8g, poly 0.4g); Protein 14.6g; Carb 21.5g; Fiber 2.9g; Chol 20mg; Iron 1.2mg; Sodium 559mg; Calc 382mg

 SERVE WITH *Whether you make this for a "soup-and-sandwich" night or a "soup-and-salad" lunch, it will be a hit! Serve with Parmesan cheese-topped broiled tomatoes.*

Savannah-Style Crab Soup

HANDS-ON TIME: 12 min. **TOTAL TIME:** 39 min.

PREP TIP *If the flour starts to brown too quickly, remove the skillet from the heat, and stir the flour constantly until it cools.*

2.25 ounces all-purpose flour (about ½ cup)
1 tablespoon butter
Cooking spray
½ (8-ounce) package shredded carrot, coarsely chopped (about 2 cups)
1 (14-ounce) package frozen chopped peppers, celery, and onion (such as Birds Eye)
1 teaspoon bottled minced garlic

1 tablespoon Old Bay seasoning
¼ teaspoon black pepper
¼ teaspoon dried thyme
1 bay leaf
4 cups clam juice
1½ cups whole milk
½ cup half-and-half
1 pound lump crabmeat, shell pieces removed
⅓ cup dry sherry

1 **Place flour in a 9-inch cast-iron skillet;** cook over medium heat 15 minutes stirring frequently until flour turns color; then stir constantly until brown. Remove from heat.

2 **While flour browns,** melt butter in a Dutch oven coated with cooking spray over medium-high heat. Add carrot, chopped pepper mixture, and garlic; sauté 5 minutes or until vegetables are tender. Add Old Bay seasoning, black pepper, dried thyme, and bay leaf; cook 1 minute. Sprinkle browned flour over vegetable mixture, and cook 1 minute, stirring frequently. Stir in clam juice, and bring mixture to a boil. Reduce heat, and simmer 10 minutes or until mixture is slightly thick, stirring frequently.

3 **Stir in milk and half-and-half;** cook 4 minutes. Stir in crabmeat and sherry; cook 5 minutes or until soup is thoroughly heated. Discard bay leaf before serving. Serves 9 (serving size: 1 cup)

Calories 151; Fat 5g (sat 2.6g; mono 1.4g, poly 0.4g); Protein 13g; Carb 13.3g; Fiber 1.8g; Chol 46mg; Iron 2.2mg; Sodium 706mg; Calc 112mg

Creamy Shrimp
and Corn Bowl

HANDS-ON TIME: 5 min. **TOTAL TIME:** 13 min.

 PREP TIP *Purchase shrimp already peeled and deveined. If your grocery store doesn't offer them, use frozen peeled and deveined shrimp, and let them thaw in the refrigerator.*

Cooking spray
1½ **pounds large shrimp, peeled and deveined**
¾ **cup chopped green onions, divided**
¼ **cup water**
¾ **teaspoon Old Bay seasoning**
1 **(11-ounce) can extra-sweet whole-kernel corn, drained**
¾ **cup half-and-half**

1 **Heat a large saucepan over medium-high heat.** Coat pan with cooking spray. Add shrimp to pan; sauté 3 minutes.

2 **Add ½ cup onions, ¼ cup water, seasoning, and corn;** bring to a boil. Cover, reduce heat, and simmer 5 minutes.

3 **Remove from heat; stir in half-and-half.** Cover; let stand 3 minutes. Sprinkle with remaining ¼ cup onions. Serves 4 (serving size: 1 cup shrimp mixture and 1 tablespoon onions)

Calories 279; Fat 8.1g (sat 3.6g; mono 1.9g, poly 1.1g); Protein 37.3g; Carb 12g; Fiber 2g; Chol 281mg; Iron 4.3mg; Sodium 594mg; Calc 149mg

 SERVE WITH *Serve with sliced baguette for dipping.*

Three-Bean Chili

HANDS-ON TIME: 5 min. **TOTAL TIME:** 18 min.

 PREP TIP *Don't be intimated by the length of the ingredient list—it calls for vegetables that can be purchased already chopped and five cans to open, making hands-on time only five minutes.*

2 teaspoons olive oil
1 cup prechopped onion
½ cup prechopped green bell pepper
2 teaspoons bottled minced garlic
¾ cup water
2 tablespoons tomato paste
2 teaspoons chili powder
2 teaspoons ground cumin
¼ teaspoon black pepper
1 (15½-ounce) can garbanzo beans, rinsed and drained
1 (15½-ounce) can red kidney beans, rinsed and drained
1 (15½-ounce) can black beans, rinsed and drained
1 (14½-ounce) can organic vegetable broth (such as Swanson Certified Organic)
1 (14½-ounce) can no-salt-added diced tomatoes, undrained
1 tablespoon yellow cornmeal
¼ cup chopped fresh cilantro
6 tablespoons reduced-fat sour cream

1 **Heat a large saucepan over medium-high heat.** Add olive oil to pan; swirl to coat. Add onion, bell pepper, and garlic to pan; sauté 3 minutes.

2 **Stir in ¾ cup water and next 9 ingredients (through diced tomatoes);** bring to a boil. Reduce heat, and simmer 8 minutes.

3 **Stir in cornmeal; cook 2 minutes.** Remove from heat; stir in cilantro. Serve with sour cream. Serves 6 (serving size: 1⅓ cups chili and 1 tablespoon sour cream)

Calories 180; Fat 4.9g (sat 1.5g, mono 1.7g, poly 0.3g); Protein 8.4g; Carb 29.5g; Fiber 8.6g; Chol 5mg; Iron 2.3mg; Sodium 644mg; Calc 86mg

 SERVE WITH *Add corn muffins to this three-bean chili recipe, and you've got yourself a meal.*

Chicken Chili

HANDS-ON TIME: 10 min. **TOTAL TIME:** 19 min.

 Be sure to mash the beans and chiles, as this helps thicken the broth for a delicious bowl of chili.

- 1 tablespoon canola oil
- 1 pound chicken breast tenders, cut into bite-sized pieces
- ³/₄ teaspoon salt, divided
- ¹/₂ cup vertically sliced onion
- 2 teaspoons bottled minced garlic
- 2 teaspoons ground cumin
- 1 teaspoon ground coriander
- ¹/₂ teaspoon dried oregano
- ¹/₄ teaspoon ground red pepper

- 3 cups no-salt-added canned cannellini beans, rinsed and drained
- 1 cup water
- 2 (4-ounce) cans chopped green chiles, undrained and divided
- 1 (14-ounce) can fat-free, lower-sodium chicken broth
- ¹/₄ cup cilantro leaves
- 1 lime, cut into 6 wedges

 Heat a Dutch oven over medium-high heat. Add oil to pan; swirl to coat. Sprinkle chicken with ¹/₄ teaspoon salt. Add chicken; sauté 4 minutes.

Add onion and next 5 ingredients (through red pepper); sauté 3 minutes. Add 2 cups beans, 1 cup water, remaining ¹/₂ teaspoon salt, 1 can chiles, and broth; bring to a boil.

 Mash 1 cup beans and 1 can chiles in a bowl. Add to soup; simmer 5 minutes. Serve with cilantro and lime. Serves 6 (serving size: 1 cup and 1 lime wedge)

Calories 189; Fat 4.3g (sat 0.5g; mono 1.8g, poly 1g); Protein 22.3g; Carb 15.1g; Fiber 4.8g; Chol 44mg; Iron 2.6mg; Sodium 624mg; Calc 67mg

Stovetop "Baked Beans," page 193

6

1-step sides »

Only minutes in the making, these tasty sides creatively marry fresh ingredients and home-style flavor.

« Balsamic Roasted Asparagus

HANDS-ON TIME: 2 min. **TOTAL TIME:** 12 min.

- - - - - - - - - -

1 pound asparagus
1 tablespoon olive oil
1 tablespoon balsamic vinegar
½ teaspoon kosher salt
½ teaspoon bottled minced garlic
¼ teaspoon freshly ground black pepper

1. Preheat oven to 425°. Snap off tough ends of asparagus. Place in a jelly-roll pan. Drizzle with olive oil and vinegar; sprinkle with salt, garlic, and pepper. Toss to coat. Bake at 425° for 10 minutes, turning once. Serves 4

Calories 67; Fat 3.6g (sat 0.5g, mono 2.7g, poly 0.3g); Protein 2.5g; Carb 5.7g; Fiber 2.5g; Chol 0mg; Iron 0.5mg; Sodium 236mg; Calc 26mg

Stovetop "Baked Beans"

(pictured on page 190)

HANDS-ON TIME: 5 min. **TOTAL TIME:** 20 min.

- - - - - - - - - -

PREP TIP *Purchasing chopped onion and bell pepper keeps prep time to a minimum. Frozen or fresh chopped vegetables will work in this quick recipe.*

1 tablespoon butter
1¼ cups prechopped onion
¾ cup prechopped green bell pepper
2 teaspoons bottled minced garlic
1 cup reduced-calorie ketchup

¼ cup packed brown sugar
¼ cup maple syrup
2 tablespoons Worcestershire sauce
2 teaspoons barbecue smoked seasoning (such as Hickory Liquid Smoke)
2 teaspoons prepared mustard
1 (16-ounce) can red beans, rinsed and drained
1 (15.8-ounce) can Great Northern beans, rinsed and drained

1. Melt butter in a medium saucepan over medium-high heat. Add onion, bell pepper, and garlic; sauté 4 minutes. Stir in ketchup and remaining ingredients; bring to a boil. Reduce heat; simmer 15 minutes, stirring occasionally. Serves 8 (serving size: ½ cup)

Calories 179; Fat 1.9g (sat 0.4g, mono 0.7g, poly 0.7g); Protein 6g; Carb 34.6g; Fiber 3.8g; Chol 0mg; Iron 2mg; Sodium 331mg; Calc 53mg

Broccoli *with* Red Pepper
« Flakes *and* Toasted Garlic

HANDS-ON TIME: 5 min. **TOTAL TIME:** 5 min.

- - - - - - - - - -

2 teaspoons olive oil
1 (12-ounce) package broccoli florets
¼ teaspoon kosher salt
¼ teaspoon crushed red pepper
1 tablespoon bottled minced garlic
¼ cup water

1. Heat a large nonstick skillet over medium-high heat. Add olive oil to pan; swirl to coat. Add broccoli, salt, red pepper, and garlic. Sauté 2 minutes. Add ¼ cup water. Cover, reduce heat to low, and cook 2 minutes or until broccoli is crisp-tender. Serves 4 (serving size: ³/₄ cup)

Calories 53; Fat 2.7g (sat 0.4g, mono 1.7g, poly 0.4g); Protein 3.3g; Carb 6.4g; Fiber 3.2g; Chol 0mg; Iron 1mg; Sodium 147mg; Calc 55mg

Broccoli, Cheese,
and Rice Casserole

HANDS-ON TIME: 5 min. **TOTAL TIME:** 20 min.

- - - - - - - - - -

Leftover cooked rice gives a jump start to prepping this recipe or you can cook instant rice in just five minutes.

2 cups cooked instant rice
½ cup prechopped onion
¼ cup fat-free milk

4 ounces light processed cheese, cubed (such as Velveeta Light)
2 tablespoons butter, softened
2 (10-ounce) packages frozen chopped broccoli, thawed and drained
1 (10³/₄-ounce) can condensed low-fat, lower-sodium cream of mushroom soup, undiluted

1. Combine all ingredients in a large bowl, and spoon into a 2-quart microwave-safe casserole. Cover and microwave at HIGH for 15 minutes or until broccoli is tender, stirring after 8 minutes. Serves 8 (serving size: ½ cup)

Calories 137; Fat 4.4g (sat 1.7g, mono 1.4g, poly 0.9g); Protein 6.6g; Carb 19.2g; Fiber 2.2g; Chol 8mg; Iron 1.1mg; Sodium 343mg; Calc 160mg

Zesty Broccoli-Cauliflower Gratin »

HANDS-ON TIME: 5 min. **TOTAL TIME:** 15 min.

- - - - - - - - - -

PREP TIP *Coarse-grained mustard is made with mustard seed that has not been ground into a powder; only half of the seeds are ground to a paste and the rest of the seeds are left whole. If you don't have it on hand, use Dijon mustard, which will provide the mustard flavor but not the pop of seeds.*

$\frac{1}{3}$ cup dry breadcrumbs
2 tablespoons finely shredded extra-sharp cheddar cheese
2 cups frozen broccoli florets
2 cups frozen cauliflower florets
Cooking spray
1 tablespoon butter, melted
1 tablespoon coarse-grained mustard
$\frac{1}{4}$ teaspoon white pepper

1. Preheat oven to 425°. Combine breadcrumbs and cheddar cheese; stir breadcrumb mixture well, and set aside. Steam broccoli and cauliflower, covered, 4 minutes or until vegetables are crisp-tender. Drain vegetables, and place in a 1½-quart casserole coated with cooking spray. Combine butter, mustard, and white pepper in a small bowl; drizzle over broccoli and cauliflower, and toss well. Sprinkle vegetables with breadcrumb mixture, and bake at 425° for 8 minutes or until thoroughly heated. Serves 4 (serving size: 1 cup)

Calories 103; Fat 5.2g (sat 2.8g, mono 1.5g, poly 0.5g); Protein 3.9g; Carb 11.3g; Fiber 2.7g; Chol 11mg; Iron 1mg; Sodium 185mg; Calc 65mg

Herbed Cauliflower

HANDS-ON TIME: 2 min. **TOTAL TIME:** 15 min.

- - - - - - - - - -

4 cups bagged prewashed cauliflower florets
1 tablespoon butter, melted
$\frac{1}{4}$ teaspoon salt
$\frac{1}{8}$ teaspoon freshly ground black pepper
2 tablespoons chopped fresh parsley

1. Cook cauliflower in boiling water 3 minutes or until crisp-tender; drain. Combine cauliflower, butter, salt, and pepper; toss to coat. Sprinkle with parsley. Serves 4 (serving size: 1 cup)

Calories 55; Fat 3.5g (sat 1.9g, mono 0.8g, poly 0.4g); Protein 2.4g; Carb 5.3g; Fiber 2.8g; Chol 8mg; Iron 0.5mg; Sodium 168mg; Calc 24mg

Lemon Pepper Veggies

HANDS-ON TIME: 2 min. **TOTAL TIME:** 6 min.

- - - - - - - - - -

PREP TIP *The frozen florets and pre-sliced carrot eliminate cleaning, cutting, and slicing the vegetables, reducing the hands-on time to only two minutes.*

2 cups frozen broccoli florets
2 cups frozen cauliflower florets
1 cup presliced carrot
1 1/2 tablespoons butter, melted
1 tablespoon unsalted lemon pepper seasoning
1/2 teaspoon garlic powder

1. Steam first 3 ingredients, covered, 5 minutes. While vegetables steam, combine butter, lemon pepper, and garlic powder in a large bowl; stir well. Add vegetables; toss gently. Serves 4 (serving size: 1 cup)

Calories 75; Fat 4.6g (sat 2.8g, mono 1.1g, poly 0.3g); Protein 2.1g; Carb 7.8g; Fiber 3.2g; Chol 11mg; Iron 0.6mg; Sodium 127mg; Calc 34mg

Green Beans *with* Bacon ›

HANDS-ON TIME: 10 min. **TOTAL TIME:** 15 min.

- - - - - - - - - -

12 ounces green beans, trimmed
2 bacon slices
1/4 cup thinly sliced shallots
1 teaspoon fresh lemon juice
1/8 teaspoon salt
1/8 teaspoon freshly ground black pepper

1. Cook green beans in boiling water 5 minutes or until crisp-tender. Drain, and plunge beans into ice water; drain. While beans cook, cook bacon in a Dutch oven over medium heat until crisp. Remove bacon from pan; crumble. Add shallots to drippings in pan; sauté 4 minutes or until tender. Add beans, juice, salt, and pepper to pan; toss to combine. Cook 5 minutes or until thoroughly heated, stirring often. Remove from heat. Sprinkle bacon over bean mixture; toss. Serves 4 (serving size: about 1 cup)

Calories 67; Fat 3.6g (sat 0.5g, mono 2.7g, poly 0.3g); Protein 2.5g; Carb 5.7g; Fiber 2.5g; Chol 0mg; Iron 0.5mg; Sodium 236mg; Calc 26mg

Almond Green Beans

HANDS-ON TIME: 6 min. **TOTAL TIME:** 10 min.

- - - - - - - - - -

Toasting the almonds in a skillet is the quickest method and gives the nuts a rich, earthy flavor.

1 tablespoon butter
¼ cup slivered almonds

2 teaspoons bottled minced garlic
12 ounces green beans, trimmed
3 tablespoons water
¼ teaspoon salt
¼ teaspoon freshly ground black pepper

1. Melt butter in a large skillet over medium heat. Add almonds; cook 2 minutes or until lightly browned, stirring constantly. Remove from pan with a slotted spoon. Add garlic to pan; cook 30 seconds, stirring constantly. Add green beans, 3 tablespoons water, salt, and pepper. Cover and cook 4 minutes or until beans are tender and liquid evaporates. Sprinkle with almonds. Serves 4 (serving size: about 1 cup)

Calories 96; Fat 6.5g (sat 2.1g, mono 2.8g, poly 1g); Protein 3.1g; Carb 8.6g; Fiber 3.6g; Chol 8mg; Iron 1mg; Sodium 174mg; Calc 59mg

« Roasted Brussels Sprouts

HANDS-ON TIME: 4 min. **TOTAL TIME:** 19 min.

- - - - - - - - - -

1 pound Brussels sprouts, trimmed and halved lengthwise
1 tablespoon olive oil
¼ teaspoon salt
¼ teaspoon freshly ground black pepper
Cooking spray
1 tablespoon balsamic glaze (such as Gia Russa)
1 teaspoon water

1. Preheat oven to 450°. Combine first 4 ingredients on a jelly-roll pan coated with cooking spray. Bake at 450° for 15 minutes or until Brussels sprouts are tender and browned, stirring occasionally. Combine balsamic glaze and 1 teaspoon water. Drizzle evenly over Brussels sprouts. Serves 4 (serving size: ³/₄ cup)

Calories 82; Fat 4g (sat 0.6g, mono 2.5g, poly 0.7g); Protein 3.5g; Carb 11g; Fiber 3.9g; Chol 0mg; Iron 1.4mg; Sodium 173mg; Calc 43mg

« Glazed Baby Carrots

HANDS-ON TIME: 5 min. **TOTAL TIME:** 10 min.

PREP TIP *Purchase peeled baby carrots for convenience, leaving only the parsley to be chopped.*

1/4 **cup water**
1/4 **cup cider vinegar**
2 1/2 **tablespoons brown sugar**

12 **ounces peeled baby carrots**
1 **tablespoon butter**
1/4 **teaspoon freshly ground black pepper**
1/8 **teaspoon salt**
1 **tablespoon chopped fresh flat-leaf parsley**

1. Combine water, vinegar, brown sugar, and carrots in a medium skillet over medium-high heat. Cover and bring to a boil. Reduce heat, and simmer 6 minutes or until carrots are crisp-tender. Increase heat to medium-high; cook 2 minutes or until liquid is syrupy. Stir in butter, pepper, and salt. Sprinkle with parsley. Serves 4 (serving size: about 2/3 cup)

Calories 92; Fat 3g (sat 1.9g, mono 0.8g, poly 0.2g); Protein 0.6g; Carb 15.8g; Fiber 2.5g; Chol 8mg; Iron 1mg; Sodium 169mg; Calc 38mg

Easy Corn Casserole

HANDS-ON TIME: 5 min. **TOTAL TIME:** 45 min.

PREP TIP *Taking only five minutes to combine, this comforting 1-step casserole is too yummy not to include. Put it in the oven while you prepare the rest of the meal, and baking time will go by quickly.*

1 **tablespoon lower-sodium soy sauce**
1/4 **cup egg substitute**

1/4 **cup butter, melted**
1 **(8 3/4-ounce) can no-salt-added whole-kernel corn, drained**
1 **(8 3/4-ounce) can no-salt-added cream-style corn**
1 **(8 1/2-ounce) package corn muffin mix**
1 **(8-ounce) carton plain fat-free yogurt**
Cooking spray

1. Preheat oven to 350°. Combine first 7 ingredients in a medium bowl; stir well. Pour into an 8-inch square baking dish coated with cooking spray. Bake at 350° for 45 minutes or until set. Serves 8

Calories 238; Fat 9.2g (sat 4.8g, mono 3g, poly 0.6g); Protein 4.9g; Carb 35.2g; Fiber 1.5g; Chol 16mg; Iron 1.3mg; Sodium 327mg; Calc 43mg

Wilted Greens *with* « Warm Bacon Dressing

HANDS-ON TIME: 6 min. **TOTAL TIME:** 6 min.

- - - - - - - - - - -

2¼ cups water, divided
½ cup frozen green peas, thawed
4 turkey bacon slices, diced
2 tablespoons red wine vinegar
2 tablespoons fresh lemon juice
6 cups gourmet salad greens (about ¼ pound)
½ cup thinly sliced green onions
Coarsely ground black pepper (optional)

1. Bring 2 cups water to a boil in a saucepan; add peas. Cover and cook 5 minutes or until crisp-tender. While peas cook, cook bacon in a nonstick skillet over medium heat 4 minutes or until crisp. Add ¼ cup water, vinegar, and lemon juice; cook 2 minutes. Drain peas, and rinse under cold running water; drain well. Combine peas, salad greens, and green onions in a bowl. Pour warm bacon mixture pour over salad, and toss gently to coat. Sprinkle each serving with pepper, if desired. Serves 4 (serving size: 1½ cups)

Calories 56; Fat 2.6g (sat 0.7g, mono 1g, poly 0.8g); Protein 4g; Carb 5.1g; Fiber 1.1g; Chol 10mg; Iron 0.5mg; Sodium 195mg; Calc 14mg

Garlic Lima Beans

HANDS-ON TIME: 2 min. **TOTAL TIME:** 17 min.

- - - - - - - - - - -

PREP TIP

When buying frozen limas, look for baby lima beans, as they'll cook faster than the larger beans.

2 cups frozen baby lima beans
2½ cups water
1 tablespoon olive oil

2 teaspoons bottled minced garlic
3 thyme sprigs
1 bay leaf
½ teaspoon sea salt
¼ teaspoon freshly ground black pepper

1. Combine first 6 ingredients in a medium saucepan. Bring to a boil. Cover, reduce heat, and simmer 15 minutes or until tender. Discard thyme sprigs and bay leaf. Stir in salt and pepper. Serves 8 (serving size: ½ cup)

Calories 105; Fat 2.4g (sat 0.4g, mono 1.3g, poly 0.5g); Protein 5.4g; Carb 16.2g; Fiber 3.9g; Chol 0mg; Iron 2.5mg; Sodium 152mg; Calc 30mg

Microwave
« Smashed Potatoes

HANDS-ON TIME: 5 min. **TOTAL TIME:** 15 min.

- - - - - - - - - -

4 **(6-ounce) baking potatoes, peeled and cut into 1-inch pieces**
½ **cup reduced-fat sour cream**
½ **cup 1% low-fat milk**
2 **tablespoons minced fresh chives**
½ **teaspoon salt**
½ **teaspoon freshly ground black pepper**

1. Place potato pieces in a large microwave-safe bowl. Cover bowl with plastic wrap; cut a 1-inch slit in center of plastic wrap. Microwave at HIGH 10 minutes. Let stand 2 minutes. Add sour cream and remaining ingredients to bowl; mash with a potato masher. Serves 4 (serving size: about 1 cup)

Calories 192; Fat 4.8g (sat 2.9g, mono 1.4g, poly 0.2g); Protein 5.8g; Carb 32.1g; Fiber 2.1g; Chol 12mg; Iron 0.5mg; Sodium 333mg; Calc 91mg

- - - - - - - - - -

Southwest Variation

Omit sour cream and chives; decrease milk to 2 tablespoons and salt to ¼ teaspoon. Add ³/₄ cup plain low-fat yogurt; 1 tablespoon chopped chipotle chile, canned in adobo sauce; and ¼ teaspoon ground cumin. Serves 4 (serving size: about 1 cup)

Calories 155; Fat 1g (sat 0.6g, mono 0.2g, poly 0.1g); Protein 5.3g; Carb 32.1g; Fiber 2.1g; Chol 3mg; Iron 0.6mg; Sodium 195mg; Calc 103mg

- - - - - - - - - -

Roasted Garlic Variation

Note: You can find roasted garlic cloves at the salad bar in many grocery stores. Omit sour cream and chives; increase milk to ³/₄ cup. Add ¼ cup coarsely chopped roasted garlic cloves and 1 tablespoon chopped fresh sage. Serves 4 (serving size: about 1 cup)

Calories 155; Fat 0.7g (sat 0.3g, mono 0.1g, poly 0.1g); Protein 4.7g; Carb 33.6g; Fiber 2.2g; Chol 2mg; Iron 0.6mg; Sodium 323mg; Calc 83mg

- - - - - - - - - -

Bacon *and* Cheddar Variation

Decrease salt to ¼ teaspoon. Add 1 ounce shredded reduced-fat extra-sharp (about ¼ cup) cheddar cheese and 1 center-cut bacon slice, cooked and crumbled; mash with a potato masher to desired consistency. Serves 4 (serving size: about 1 cup)

Calories 218; Fat 6.6g (sat 4.0g, mono 1.7g, poly 0.3g); Protein 8.3g; Carb 32g; Fiber 2.1g; Chol 18mg; Iron 0.6mg; Sodium 274mg; Calc 155mg

Maple-Bacon
« Mashed Sweet Potatoes

HANDS-ON TIME: 7 min. **TOTAL TIME:** 15 min.

- - - - - - - - - -

4 sweet potatoes (about 2 pounds)
1 tablespoon softened butter
2 tablespoons fat-free milk
4 teaspoons maple syrup
1¼ ounces cooked and crumbled bacon (about 3 slices)

1. Pierce each potato with a fork 3 to 4 times on each side. Wrap each potato in a damp paper towel. Microwave at HIGH 8 minutes, turning after 4 minutes. Cool slightly. Cut potatoes in half; scoop pulp into a bowl. Mash pulp. Stir butter, milk, and syrup into potato pulp. Top with bacon. Serves 4 (serving size: ½ cup)

Calories 228; Fat 6.8g (sat 3.1g, mono 2.4g, poly 0.6g); Protein 6g; Carb 36.3g; Fiber 4.4g; Chol 18mg; Iron 1.4mg; Sodium 282mg; Calc 66mg

Steamed Sugar Snap Peas

HANDS-ON TIME: 3 min. **TOTAL TIME:** 8 min.

- - - - - - - - - -

PREP TIP

Fresh tarragon can be used in place of mint for an anise-like flavor.

3 cups fresh sugar snap peas
1 tablespoon chopped fresh mint
1 tablespoon butter
⅛ teaspoon salt
⅛ teaspoon freshly ground black pepper

1. Steam peas 5 minutes or until crisp-tender; drain. Combine peas, mint, butter, salt, and pepper; toss well. Serves 4 (serving size: ¾ cup)

Calories 46; Fat 3g (sat 1.8g, mono 0.8g, poly 0.2g); Protein 1.4g; Carb 3.7g; Fiber 1.3g; Chol 8mg; Iron 1mg; Sodium 96mg; Calc 22mg

Classic Apple *and* Blue Cheese Salad

HANDS-ON TIME: 15 min. **TOTAL TIME:** 15 min.

- - - - - - - - - -

2 tablespoons fresh lemon juice

2 teaspoons sugar

1½ teaspoons extra-virgin olive oil

2 teaspoons Dijon mustard

¼ teaspoon salt

¼ teaspoon freshly ground black pepper

6 cups torn Bibb lettuce leaves (about 2 heads)

1 cup chopped Granny Smith apple

2 tablespoons crumbled blue cheese

2 tablespoons chopped green onions

1 tablespoon chopped toasted walnuts

1. Combine first 6 ingredients in a large bowl, stirring with a whisk. Add lettuce and remaining ingredients, tossing gently to coat. Serves 6 (serving size: about ¾ cup)

Calories 54; Fat 2.9g (sat 0.6g, mono 1.2g, poly 0.8g); Protein 1.7g; Carb 6.5g; Fiber 1.3g; Chol 1.8mg; Iron 0.3mg; Sodium 176mg; Calc 35mg

Arugula Salad *with* Caesar Vinaigrette »

HANDS-ON TIME: 5 min. **TOTAL TIME:** 5 min.

- - - - - - - - - -

PREP TIP

Leftover anchovies can be stored in a tightly sealed container in the refrigerator.

2 tablespoons extra-virgin olive oil

½ teaspoon grated lemon rind

2 teaspoons fresh lemon juice

⅛ teaspoon freshly ground black pepper

2 chopped canned anchovy fillets

1 teaspoon bottled minced garlic

4 cups arugula

2 tablespoons shaved fresh Parmesan cheese

1. Combine first 6 ingredients in a medium bowl, stirring with a whisk. Add arugula; toss to coat. Sprinkle with shaved fresh Parmesan cheese. Serves 4 (serving size: about 1 cup)

Calories 82; Fat 7.8g (sat 1.4g, mono 5.2g, poly 0.9g); Protein 2.1g; Carb 1.3g; Fiber 0.4g; Chol 4mg; Iron .5mg; Sodium 117mg; Calc 67mg

Warm Spinach Salad

HANDS-ON TIME: 5 min. **TOTAL TIME:** 5 min.

- - - - - - - - -

6 cups baby spinach leaves
2 tablespoons olive oil
1 teaspoon bottled minced garlic
½ cup grape tomatoes
2 tablespoons cider vinegar
1 teaspoon honey
½ teaspoon black pepper
¼ teaspoon salt

1. Place spinach leaves in a large bowl. Heat a small skillet over medium-high heat. Add olive oil; swirl to coat. Add garlic and tomatoes; cook 1 minute, stirring constantly. Add vinegar, honey, pepper, and salt, stirring with a whisk. Add vinegar mixture to spinach; toss to coat. Serves 4 (serving size: 1 cup)

Calories 87; Fat 6.8g (sat 0.9g, mono 4.9g, poly 0.7g); Protein 1.1g; Carb 6.5g; Fiber 2g; Chol 0mg; Iron 1.3mg; Sodium 207mg; Calc 31mg

---

« Parsley-Spinach Salad

HANDS-ON TIME: 5 min. **TOTAL TIME:** 5 min.

- - - - - - - - -

PREP TIP

Hyperspeed this super-simple salad by using prewashed bagged baby spinach.

1 tablespoon fresh lemon juice
1 tablespoon olive oil
¼ teaspoon salt

¼ teaspoon freshly ground black pepper
¼ teaspoon Dijon mustard
5 cups baby spinach leaves
1 cup flat-leaf parsley leaves
3 tablespoons chopped pistachios

1. Combine first 5 ingredients in a medium bowl. Add spinach and parsley; toss to coat. Top with pistachios. Serves 4 (serving size: 1 cup)

Calories 82; Fat 6.1g (sat 0.8g, mono 3.9g, poly 1.2g); Protein 2.4g; Carb 6.3g; Fiber 2.6g; Chol 0mg; Iron 2.2mg; Sodium 212mg; Calc 49mg

Asian Slaw

HANDS-ON TIME: 6 min. **TOTAL TIME:** 6 min.

PREP TIP

Dark sesame oil is toasted sesame oil, and has a stronger flavor than regular sesame oil. You can use regular sesame oil for this recipe if you prefer a milder flavor.

$1/4$ cup canola mayonnaise
1 tablespoon lower-sodium soy sauce
1 teaspoon dark sesame oil
4 cups packaged 3-color coleslaw (such as Fresh Express)
$1/2$ cup chopped fresh cilantro

1. Combine first 3 ingredients in a medium bowl, stirring with a whisk. Add coleslaw and cilantro; toss well. Serves 4 (serving size: $3/4$ cup)

Calories 46; Fat 3.2g (sat 0.2g, mono 0.5g, poly 1.5g); Protein 0.8g; Carb 4.8g; Fiber 1.1g; Chol 0mg; Iron 0.2mg; Sodium 290mg; Calc 21mg

---

« Cilantro-Chipotle Rice

HANDS-ON TIME: 2 min. **TOTAL TIME:** 6 min.

---

1 (10-ounce) package frozen brown rice (such as Birds Eye)
$1/3$ cup bottle chipotle salsa
$1/4$ cup chopped fresh cilantro

1. Heat rice according to package directions. Transfer rice to a medium bowl. Stir in salsa and cilantro. Serve immediately. Serves 4 (serving size: $1/2$ cup)

Calories 85; Fat 1g (sat 0.1g, mono 0.2g, poly 0.2g); Protein 2.1 g; Carb 17.5g; Fiber 1.6g; Chol 0mg; Iron 0.mg; Sodium 156mg; Calc 11mg

« Herbed Parmesan Capellini

HANDS-ON TIME: 5 min. **TOTAL TIME:** 8 min.

- - - - - - - - - -

 PREP TIP *Other shaped pastas can be used; increase the cooking time per package directions.*

4 ounces uncooked capellini or angel hair pasta
1 tablespoon olive oil

1 tablespoon chopped fresh parsley
2 teaspoons chopped fresh oregano
1/8 teaspoon salt
1/8 teaspoon freshly ground black pepper
1 ounce shaved fresh Parmesan cheese (about 1/4 cup)

1. Cook pasta according to package directions, omitting salt and fat. Drain pasta, and place in a large bowl. Add olive oil and next 4 ingredients (through pepper); toss to coat. Place pasta on each of 4 plates. Sprinkle each evenly with cheese. Serves 4 (serving size: 1/2 cup pasta and 1 tablespoon cheese)

Calories 176; Fat 6.5g (sat 2.3g, mono 3.4g, poly 0.6g); Protein 7.7g; Carb 21.7g; Fiber 0.9g; Chol 7mg; Iron 1.1mg; Sodium 317mg; Cal 135mg

Lemon Couscous

HANDS-ON TIME: 5 min. **TOTAL TIME:** 5 min.

- - - - - - - - - -

1 1/4 cups water
3/4 cup uncooked couscous
1/4 cup sliced green onions
2 tablespoons finely chopped fresh parsley

2 tablespoons orange juice
1 teaspoon grated lemon rind
1 tablespoon fresh lemon juice
1/4 teaspoon salt
1/8 teaspoon black pepper

1. Bring 1 1/4 cups water to a boil in a medium saucepan; gradually stir in couscous. Remove from heat; cover and let stand 5 minutes. Fluff with a fork. Stir in onions and remaining ingredients. Serves 4 (serving size: 1/2 cup)

Calories 102; Fat 0.3g (sat 0.0g, mono 0.0g, poly 0.0g); Protein 3.7g; Carb 21.8g; Fiber 1.3g; Chol 0mg; Iron 0.8mg; Sodium 151mg; Calc 9mg

Nutritional Analysis

How to Use It and Why

Glance at the end of any *Cooking Light* recipe, and you'll see how committed we are to helping you make the best of today's light cooking. With chefs, registered dietitians, home economists, and a computer system that analyzes every ingredient we use, *Cooking Light* gives you authoritative dietary detail like no other magazine. We go to such lengths so you can see how our recipes fit into your healthful eating plan. If you're trying to lose weight, the calorie and fat figures will probably help most. But if you're keeping a close eye on the sodium, cholesterol, and saturated fat in your diet, we provide those numbers, too. And because many women don't get enough iron or calcium, we can help there, as well. Finally, there's a fiber analysis for those of us who don't get enough roughage.

Here's a helpful guide to put our nutritional analysis numbers into perspective. Remember, one size doesn't fit all, so take your lifestyle, age, and circumstances into consideration when determining your nutrition needs. For example, pregnant or breast-feeding women need more protein, calories, and calcium. And women older than 50 need 1,200mg of calcium daily, 200mg more than the amount recommended for younger women.

In Our Nutritional Analysis, We Use These Abbreviations

sat saturated fat	CARB carbohydrates	g gram
mono monounsaturated fat	CHOL cholesterol	mg milligram
poly polyunsaturated fat	CALC calcium	

Daily Nutrition Guide

	Women ages 25 to 50	Women over 50	Men ages 24 to 50	Men over 50
Calories	2,000	2,000 or less	2,700	2,500
Protein	50g	50g or less	63g	60g
Fat	65g or less	65g or less	88g or less	83g or less
Saturated Fat	20g or less	20g or less	27g or less	25g or less
Carbohydrates	304g	304g	410g	375g
Fiber	25g to 35g	25g to 35g	25g to 35g	25g to 35g
Cholesterol	300mg or less	300mg or less	300mg or less	300mg or less
Iron	18mg	8mg	8mg	8mg
Sodium	2,300mg or less	1,500mg or less	2,300mg or less	1,500mg or less
Calcium	1,000mg	1,200mg	1,000mg	1,000mg

The nutritional values used in our calculations either come from The Food Processor, Version 10.4 (ESHA Research), or are provided by food manufacturers.

Metric Equivalents

The information in the following charts is provided to help cooks outside the United States successfully use the recipes in this book. All equivalents are approximate.

Cooking/Oven Temperatures

	Fahrenheit	Celsius	Gas Mark
Freeze Water	32° F	0° C	
Room Temp.	68° F	20° C	
Boil Water	212° F	100° C	
Bake	325° F	160° C	3
	350° F	180° C	4
	375° F	190° C	5
	400° F	200° C	6
	425° F	220° C	7
	450° F	230° C	8
Broil			Grill

Liquid Ingredients by Volume

¼ tsp	=					1 ml		
½ tsp	=					2 ml		
1 tsp	=					5 ml		
3 tsp	=	1 Tbsp	=	½ fl oz	=	15 ml		
2 Tbsp	=	⅛ cup	=	1 fl oz	=	30 ml		
4 Tbsp	=	¼ cup	=	2 fl oz	=	60 ml		
5⅓ Tbsp	=	⅓ cup	=	3 fl oz	=	80 ml		
8 Tbsp	=	½ cup	=	4 fl oz	=	120 ml		
10⅔ Tbsp	=	⅔ cup	=	5 fl oz	=	160 ml		
12 Tbsp	=	¾ cup	=	6 fl oz	=	180 ml		
16 Tbsp	=	1 cup	=	8 fl oz	=	240 ml		
1 pt	=	2 cups	=	16 fl oz	=	480 ml		
1 qt	=	4 cups	=	32 fl oz	=	960 ml		
				33 fl oz	=	1000 ml	=	1 l

Dry Ingredients by Weight

(To convert ounces to grams, multiply the number of ounces by 30.)

1 oz	=	1/16 lb	=	30 g
4 oz	=	¼ lb	=	120 g
8 oz	=	½ lb	=	240 g
12 oz	=	¾ lb	=	360 g
16 oz	=	1 lb	=	480 g

Equivalents for Different Types of Ingredients

Standard Cup	Fine Powder (ex. flour)	Grain (ex. rice)	Granular (ex. sugar)	Liquid Solids (ex. butter)	Liquid (ex. milk)
1	140 g	150 g	190 g	200 g	240 ml
¾	105 g	113 g	143 g	150 g	180 ml
⅔	93 g	100 g	125 g	133 g	160 ml
½	70 g	75 g	95 g	100 g	120 ml
⅓	47 g	50 g	63 g	67 g	80 ml
¼	35 g	38 g	48 g	50 g	60 ml
⅛	18 g	19 g	24 g	25 g	30 ml

Length

(To convert inches to centimeters, multiply the number of inches by 2.5.)

1 in	=			2.5 cm	
6 in	=	½ ft	=	15 cm	
12 in	=	1 ft	=	30 cm	
36 in	=	3 ft	= 1 yd =	90 cm	
40 in	=			100 cm	= 1 m

INDEX

©2014 by Time Home Entertainment Inc.
135 West 50th Street, New York, NY 10020

ISBN-13: 978-0-8487-4241-6
ISBN-10: 0-8487-4241-9

Library of Congress Control Number: 2014938999
Printed in the United States of America
First Printing 2014

Oxmoor House

Editorial Director: Leah McLaughlin
Creative Director: Felicity Keane
Art Director: Christopher Rhoads
Executive Food Director: Grace Parisi
Senior Editor: Andrea C. Kirkland, M.S., R.D.
Managing Editor: Elizabeth Tyler Austin
Assistant Managing Editor: Jeanne de Lathouder

Cooking Light 3-Step Express Comfort Food
Designer: Maribeth Jones
Assistant Test Kitchen Manager: Alyson Moreland Haynes
Recipe Testers and Developers: Tamara Goldis, R.D.;
   Stefanie Maloney; Callie Nash; Karen Rankin;
   Wendy Treadwell, R.D.; Leah Van Deren
Food Stylists: Victoria E. Cox, Margaret Monroe Dickey,
   Catherine Crowell Steele
Photography Director: Jim Bathie
Senior Photographer: Hélène Dujardin
Senior Photo Stylists: Kay E. Clarke, Mindi Shapiro Levine
Senior Production Managers: Greg A. Amason, Sue Chodakiewicz

Contributors
Editor: Cathy Wesler, R.D.
Project Editor: Melissa Brown
Compositor: Teresa Cole
Copy Editors: Adrienne Davis, Jacqueline Giovanelli
Proofreader: Barry Smith
Indexer: Nanette Cardon
Fellows: Ali Carruba, Elizabeth Laseter, Anna Ramia, Deanna Sakal,
   April Smitherman, Megan Thompson, Tonya West, Amanda Widis
Food Stylist: Erica Hopper
Photo Stylists: Mary Clayton Carl, Lydia Pursell

Cooking Light®
Editor: Scott Mowbray
Creative Director: Dimity Jones
Executive Managing Editor: Phillip Rhodes
Executive Editor, Food: Ann Taylor Pittman
Executive Editor, Digital: Allison Long Lowery
Senior Food Editors: Timothy Q. Cebula, Cheryl Slocum
Senior Editor: Cindy Hatcher
Nutrition Editor: Sidney Fry, M.S., R.D.
Associate Editor: Hannah Klinger
Assistant Editor: Kimberly Holland
Assistant Food Editor: Darcy Lenz
Test Kitchen Manager: Tiffany Vickers Davis
Recipe Testers and Developers: Robin Bashinsky,
   Adam Hickman, Deb Wise
Art Directors: Rachel Cardina Lasserre, Sheri Wilson
Designer: Hagen Stegall
Assistant Designer: Nicole Gerrity
Tablet Designer: Daniel Boone
Photo Editor: Amy Delaune
Senior Photographer: Randy Mayor
Chief Food Stylist: Kellie Gerber Kelley
Assistant Prop Stylists: Lindsey Lower, Claire Spollen
Food Styling Assistant: Blakeslee Wright Giles
Production Director: Liz Rhoades
Production Editor: Hazel R. Eddins
Production Coordinator: Christina Harrison
Copy Director: Susan Roberts McWilliams
Copy Editor: Kate Johnson
Office Manager: Alice Summerville
CookingLight.com Editor: Mallory Daugherty Brasseale
CookingLight.com Assistant Editor/Producer: Michelle Klug
Contributors: David Bonom; Katherine Brooking, R.D.;
   Maureen Callahan; Melissa Haskin; Sarah Hudgins;
   Frances Largeman-Roth, R.D.; Marge Perry;
   Allison Fishman Task
Produce Guru: Robert Schueller
Garden Gurus: Mary Beth and David Shaddix

Time Home Entertainment Inc.
President and Publisher: Jim Childs
Vice President, Finance: Vandana Patel
Executive Director, Marketing Services: Carol Pittard
Executive Director, Retail & Special Sales: Tom Mifsud
Publishing Director: Megan Pearlman
Assistant General Counsel: Simone Procas

Cover: Tomato and Asparagus "Carbonara" (page 122),
Pan-Grilled Chicken with Vegetable Relish (page 24) and
Pizza Margherita (page 104)
Page 2: Chicken Parmigiana (page 21)